The City of Wandering and Wondering

Celebrating my favourite City of London historical, literary and architectural gems.

Jerry Dowlen

Nowadays the remarkable people are those who don't write books.
EMILY HAHN (1944)

INDEX

Wandering and Wondering In The City of London — 7

NAMES AND PLACES
Taxi! — 14
Aldgate, Spitalfields & Whitechapel — 17
St Botolph — 23
Lombard Street — 26
Cheapside — 28
Fish Street Hill — 30
America Square — 34
Holborn and Blackfriars — 37
Old Father Thames — 45
North London — 52
Freedom Pass — 58
London by the Sea — 62

PEOPLE
Geoffrey Chaucer and John Betjeman — 74
Daniel Defoe — 78
William Wordsworth — 83
Blue Plaques and Statues — 87

FINANCE
Manley Hopkins — 98
Poetry in the City — 105
City Cartoons — 108
What's in a (Lloyd's) Name? — 112
Tower 42 — 117

CITY LITERARY
Lloyd's Log — 122
London Evening Papers — 126
Save Our Libraries! — 129
Speaker's Corner at Tower Hill — 133
Poem — 138

COPYRIGHT NOTICE

Copyright © 2013 Jerry Dowlen. All rights reserved.

No part of this document may be reproduced or transmitted in any form or by any means, electronic, mechanical, photocopying, recording, or otherwise, without the prior written permission of the Author.

THE CITY OF LONDON

Information Note:
The City of London is one of the oldest and most historic districts of the capital city of London. In the first century AD it was the original Roman settlement of *Londinium*. It thrived in the Middle Ages as a trading post and important port. Today its many ancient buildings, monuments and street names provide visible evidence of the City's long and fascinating history. Although today the City has only 7,000 permanent residents, its streets and buildings become busily filled by many thousands of "nine to five" commuters on working days, for the City of London is the world's biggest financial centre. In addition to this the City annually plays host to large contingents of visitors and tourists who come to see its many famous sights such as the Bank of England, The Guildhall, Lloyd's of London, London Bridge, Mansion House, The Monument, St Paul's Cathedral, Tower Bridge and the Tower of London.

WANDERING AND WONDERING IN THE CITY OF LONDON

My love affair with the City of London began in October 1966 when I started work there at the age of eighteen. I spent the next forty-six years working in the Lloyd's and London insurance market, starting and ending, incidentally, in buildings that stood right next door to each other in Leadenhall Street, EC3. My first two employers were the reinsurance broking firms Alexander Howden and Winchester Bowring. (Today they would respectively be known as Aon and Marsh). After that I worked for CNA, and finally for Ace at Lloyd's.

By the time of February 2013 when I retired from my insurance career, I had certainly "wandered" all round the City of London. I had "wondered" a lot, too.

Much of my "wandering" was in execution of my Monday to Friday insurance job. This in large part confined me to the short radius of streets that surround the Lloyd's of London building in Lime Street, EC3. (Lloyd's and the London insurance market is the world's leading centre of insurance and reinsurance. Several thousand brokers, underwriters and staff work in the market). But at lunchtimes, evenings after work and even at weekends in my own spare time, I found plenty of reasons to "wander" through the entire length and breadth of the City – north, south, east and west of my anchor-point at Lloyd's of Lime Street. I did this in pursuit of various cultural, social, shopping or sight-seeing activities.

As for the "wondering" – well, I did that in two different senses of the word.

My perambulations in the City were accompanied by a perpetual sense of wonderment at the majesty of its many magnificent buildings and monuments, its soaring skyscapes and its numerous captivating little nooks and crannies. My feeling of admiration never grew stale. Indeed, in the final years of my working career I found myself marvelling at my surroundings with even greater intensity than before. For in addition to continuing to entertain me with the sight of its oldest and grandest buildings like the College of Arms in Queen Victoria Street, the City revealed new and intriguing wonders to me as I gained greater knowledge of it from the superb 'London Collection' of books at the Barbican Library and from other information sources.

I "wondered" in the inquisitive sense, too. The City has an abundance of majesty but it also abounds in mystery. In hindsight I can see that in the busiest (early and middle) years of my working career I had little time and in all honesty little inclination to investigate and resolve the numerous puzzling thoughts that would flicker through my mind while I was buzzing around attending meetings, jumping in and out of taxis or being wined and dined. ("Hardly anyone lives in the City, so why are there so many churches?" - "Why is there a street called French Ordinary Court? What an extraordinary name!" - "If we have got a Fish Street Hill, why do we also have an Old Fish Street Hill?").

Availing myself of the fortunate luxury of winding down my office career at a less frenetic pace than I started it, I managed after 2007 to allocate some dedicated quality time for getting to know the City of London in more detail, during my working week.

And so I come to the basic rationale of this book of mine. Dear Reader, if you agree with me that the words that you can find on City street signs or on City buildings are a magic in themselves: if you feel the same stirring joy that I do when encountering a 'St James Garlickhythe in Vintry Ward', a 'Saint Andrew By-The-Wardrobe' or a 'Churchyard of St Ghastly Grim': please come for the ride with me in this book!

For this book does not set out to be a comprehensive, text-book guide to the City of London, encompassing every part of its twenty-five wards whose alphabetical names begin with Aldersgate and end with Walbrook. I seek simply to celebrate with you my own personal favourites of a few of the City's very large collection of historical, literary and architectural gems. And if I need some help to twist your arm to share my belief that a 'Ward of Bridge and Bridge Without' encountered on a City of London church-board is a beauty and a treasure in itself for its sheer shimmering alliteration and sound, let me call upon the acclaimed author Philip Pullman! For he has told us that his all-consuming addiction to words stemmed from his singing hymns at school and coming across such wonderful words as 'pavilioned in splendour and girded with praise'. He explained: "You are not sure what it means. But it feels lovely and it sounds great. It is there to be enjoyed."

City Signs and City Wards.

Here is some information about City signs and the City wards.

The distinctive sign of the City of London is its coat of arms: the two dragons holding a shield and helmet, with the motto *Domine Dirige Nos* (O Lord, direct us).

You'll see this coat of arms everywhere in the City. It is prolific in its adornment of street signs, walls of buildings and other places. For orientation it's the most simple and reliable marker of City of London territory. If you want to know that you are definitely inside 'The Square Mile' (as the City is colloquially known) it's easy! - just look for the name of the street and see whether the familiar coat of arms decorates the nameplate.

For boundary-marking the coat of arms is sounder than using the ecclesiastical option to check your bearings. By this I mean that if I tell you that St Dunstan-in-the-West in Fleet Street is the westernmost church in the City of London, closely abutting Chancery Lane in Holborn where the street signs suddenly become postal district WC2, don't jump to the conclusion that St Dunstan-in-the-East must therefore be the easternmost church in the City! For that tag belongs to St Botolph, Aldgate where the

City starts to wave hello to Whitechapel, and beyond that, the districts of Poplar, Stepney and indeed, Essex.

The City has lots of tricks up its sleeve and mysteries for us to unravel. One of them is its nickname of 'The Square Mile'. The proper rationale for the nickname is that the entire City of London occupies an area that approximately measures a square mile. To add confusion, however, the so-called Financial District of the City is also known as 'The Square Mile'. This is not really accurate: it is certainly true that the City houses a very large number of banks, insurance companies and other financial institutions, but for the most part they are all clustered around the relatively small area of the City that notably includes Leadenhall Street, Lime Street and Threadneedle Street.

The City of London dates back to Roman times and still offers us visible evidence of this heritage. Parts of the Roman wall have survived, and when we see such names as Aldgate ("Old Gate") they remind us that the City had zealously-guarded ancient privileges, most especially for trading, that grew its prosperity.

The historical blue squares are another of the City's eye-catching and distinctive features. No, please, football fans, don't get excited: I don't mean the Blue Square Conference: I am talking of the information signs that are dotted around the City and are white lettering on glazed blue tiles that have a square shape. You'll see them all around, on walls, and in true "X marks the spot" style they will impart interesting little smatterings of historical information.

In large part the signs record the former site of a church, a hospital, a livery company, a school, or other types of notable buildings and structures. For example, if you are in the street that is appropriately named London Wall – you might be on your way to or from the most excellent London Museum, near to the Barbican – you'll pass a blue sign telling you that Moor Gate (nowadays Moorgate) was demolished in 1761; turn the corner into Aldersgate Street and you'll learn from another sign that Aldersgate was taken down in the same year, too. 'Go West' – with or without the Pet Shop Boys! – and when you reach Ludgate, along from St Paul's Cathedral, you'll see that the demolition squad was busy there in 1760. Of course, when you note that the modern-day City of London occupies territory that is even further west than Ludgate –evidence of this includes a blue square sign in Fleet Street that commemorates 'The Old Serjeants' Inn' – you'll deduce that the City has expanded beyond the original confinements of its Roman wall. Its scope in fact began to creep outside the wall in medieval times, most especially to the west where it crossed the River Fleet.

You may already have guessed that I'm now going to confess that I am hopelessly smitten with the many wonderful names and words that I've found on the City's blue square signs. For example: The church of 'St Benet Sherehog'; the churches of 'All Hallows the Great' and 'All Hallows the Less'; the 'Poulters' Hall'; Sir Ebenezer Howard; the 'Giltspur Street Compter'! (Excuse me? What on earth is – or was – the 'Giltspur Street Compter'? Answer: A debtors' prison.)

I am also prone to word-worship the City's frequently-sighted wall-plaques that are oval in shape and display City ward locations in black lettering on a white background. Typical names are: 'Ward of Castle Langbourn', 'Ward of Cordwainer', 'Ward of Portsoken'. Altogether the City has twenty-five administrative wards, and some of them have the most glorious names: Bread Street, Broad Street; Candlewick, Farringdon Within, Farringdon Without, Vintry. (Shades of the nursery-rhyme: 'Butcher, Baker, Candlewick-Maker …'?).

Having made mention of the old Roman wall and the City wards, I had better pause to explain that these give evidence of the City of London enjoying still its ancient and unique self-run style of local government. The wards are survivors of the medieval governmental system that granted status to the City of a self-governing district. Even in recent history the City has sometimes been given a "bye" from legislation enacted upon its neighbouring thirty-two boroughs of Greater London. Its main instrument of government is the City of London Corporation which sub-divides into the now largely ceremonial Court of Aldermen and the more "hands-on" Court of Common Council.

If you find on some pages of this book that there is a distinct Lloyd's of London insurance slant to my descriptions of the City of London, will you please forgive me? It is inevitable that I see the City at least partly through the filter of my profession of forty-six years. And if it is my tenet that the wonderful words seen and found around the City are a kind-of living poetry in themselves, you'll see that I use this book on occasions to advocate that the bubble of Lloyd's insurance houses some fine words and poetry too!

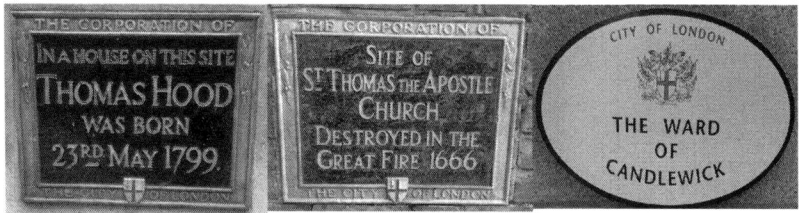

NAMES AND PLACES

Ludgate Hill with part of St Paul's Cathedral on the right.

TAXI!

What an exciting new planet it was for me to explore and get to know after I landed in the City of London in October 1966. Taxi-driver turned author Maurice Levinson had described the terrain in his book 'Taxi!' published by Secker & Warburg in 1963, and what a frightening list of places it was that a cabbie had to know then, and now, in 'The Square Mile'. ML realised that in addition to knowing where to find all of the City's famous tourist attractions such as the Tower of London, the cabbie must be familiar with the offices of all the shipping companies and the banks and insurance companies.

One rewrite of his book that ML would have to make nowadays is to cease always referring to a taxi-driver as "he". I'm not sure how ML would have reacted to females being allowed to drive cabs? – and I wonder whether he would believe the statisticians at Lloyd's insurance who declare that women are the safest drivers? His verdict on female drivers in 1963 was that they never know which way they want to go and they take too long to make up their minds; he made the accusation too that they don't know their left from their right!

If I were tested on "The Knowledge", the daunting exam that forces cabbies to store an intricate road map in their heads, my weak point in the City would be the Livery Companies: I wouldn't call them secretive exactly, but bearing in mind that there are more than a hundred of these institutions such as The Worshipful Company of Wax Chandlers, I can count on one hand the number of times that I have seen inside any of their plush, baronial banqueting suites such as Clothworkers Hall and Grocers Hall. It is a pity, I declare, that the public rarely gets a chance to pass beneath resplendent coats of arms, to ascend ornate staircases and see the rich panoply of oil-paintings, tapestries, suits of armour, silverware and glassware that many of these noble guilds have squirreled away since their medieval heydays as powerful trade associations in the City.

When I first worked in London, visitors from Britain and abroad would enthuse: "Your London policemen are wonderful"; so too our taxi-drivers, and our red buses. As of today I'm not sure about the police, but I will warrant that our taxi-drivers are still a marvel: the best in the world. I remember the radio presenter James Whale saying once that if he were Prime Minister, he would fill his Cabinet with London taxi-drivers "because they are the only people who really know what is going on in this country." There is a grain of truth in that, for sure.

If you want to search the internet for all the latest on the British press and the Leveson Enquiry, be careful with your touch-typing: you might get Maurice Levinson, instead! If you do, I think it will be a lucky accident: yes, even for lady readers, if they are willing to forgive the characteristic male chauvinism of his time that ML displayed when writing of their standard of driving. Levinson was an engaging writer; a self-taught one, for he had grown up with little education and was near-illiterate. In his autobiography 'The Woman from Bessarabia' (1964) he recounted his upbringing amidst intolerable poverty and hardship on the eastern fringe of the City. As a young man he found that it was a long hard slog to get his cabbies' badge: in his book 'Taxi!' he recalled a hilarious failure by one of his friends to pass the notoriously difficult oral exam. His friend's memory dried up, alas, in mid-route just as he had turned his imaginary cab into Tower Bridge Road. With the examiner patiently waiting, he broke the awkward silence by gallantly offering: "I'm afraid sir that I can't proceed any further, for the bridge is up." A nice try! – but he didn't pass the exam!

Maurice Levinson noted that churches are much more difficult for cabbies to find than pubs. Specifically for the City of London he referenced that there are very many churches – some of them hundreds of years old; as regards the City's pubs and indeed all its streets he knew that they have many fascinating histories, especially those that are connected with Charles Dickens. If you fire the question at me: "Which are the City of London's most famous pubs?" I will likely suggest Dirty Dick's (Bishopsgate), The Dickens Inn (St Katherine's Dock) and The Lamb (Leadenhall Market). But I know that City workers can be fiercely proprietorial about their favourite pub: stop twenty of them in the street and ask them the same question and you'll probably hear twenty different nominations, and each time the declarer will insist that his pub is <u>the</u> pub in the City.

ALDGATE, SPITALFIELDS & WHITECHAPEL

For the first ten years of my working life in the City of London (commencing in 1966) my office building was in close reach of Aldgate – the gateway to the East End.

I am not sure how I regarded the East End in those days. What was the extent of my knowledge? Did I bracket it simply with the Old Kent Road, its sister brown square on the Monopoly board, representatives both of London's most deprived areas where property was dirt cheap because hardly anyone would want to live there? Did I think of the East End as the manor of the Kray twins, where men wore shiny blue suits, called the police "rozzers" and said "tea leaf" when they meant "thief"? Was it much later in my life that I began to take on board the East End's fascinating kaleidoscope of cultural and political history – for example the Sidney Street siege in 1911 and the Cable Street riots in 1936?

I suspect that in those early days I was content to take Aldgate and Whitechapel at face value, and to marvel silently at its visible panorama of street markets (Petticoat Lane), whelk stalls (Tubby Isaacs), rag trade sweatshops, wholesale distributors (clothes, fancy goods), the Houndsditch Warehouse, Blooms restaurant, tramps, doss houses, alleys and mean streets.

In hindsight I can see that these were simply the first pieces of a giant jigsaw that would eventually extend to embrace for me the areas of Spitalfields and Brick Lane, This came in the mid-1980s when I worked in an office building on the borders of the City of London and Shoreditch. I began to explore on foot the adjacent Spitalfields Market and the streets beyond. Little by little I absorbed knowledge of the area's compelling history of immigrant settlers (Huguenots, Irish, Jews). I discovered many true-life "rags to riches" stories, for example the showbiz stars Bud Flanagan, Lew Grade. I was reminded too that Geoffrey Chaucer lived in lodgings near Aldgate and no doubt observed there many of the characters whom he described in 'The Canterbury Tales', for in Chaucer's medieval times the east-facing Aldgate was an especially busy conduit into and out of the City.

Rachel Lichtenstein has established herself as a foremost chronicler of Brick Lane's social history. Her book 'On Brick Lane' (Hamilton, 2007) is an absorbing and informative read. It is vigorously researched and factual, but nevertheless highly entertaining. In contrast, Tarquin Hall's book 'Salaam Brick Lane' (John Murray, 2006) is a funny, irreverent and knockabout sketch of Brick Lane, drawn from his experiences and observations as a temporary resident.

The best lines in 'Salaam Brick Lane' belong to the wheeler-dealer landlord Mr Ali, who crackles with every prejudice and criminal tendency under the sun, conveyed in hilarious pidgin English that requires him to end every sentence with the word "innit". The book brings it home to me moreover that during my forty-six years of working in the City of London, the next-door district of Aldgate and Whitechapel has seen a complete ethnic transformation. The presence of Jewish traders is history now. For the colour, noise and odour (malodour?) of Brick Lane will instantly reveal to you that the population of the "new" East End comes from Afghanistan, Bangladesh, India, Pakistan and Somalia.

The best book that I have read about Spitalfields is 'This Bright Field' (Methuen, 2001). The author William Taylor dabbled in a white collar job like mine in the City of London during his voyage of self-discovery towards ordination as a priest. His book is a memoir of his time living and working in Spitalfields and interacting with the local community. If I enjoyed reading his bitter-sweet observations with a special interest, this was probably due to a fancy that I could see in the young William Taylor something of myself when I worked near Spitalfields and I roved around the district during my free time in lunch hours or after work.

It takes only a moment for me to put myself in reverse gear and to find myself in the 1980s walking once more through the old Spitalfields market with its unique (but not unpleasant) smell of rotting fruit in my nostrils. If I was heading towards The Gun public house for a drink with an office colleague, or to the London Fruit Exchange where our office staff had membership of an indoor sports club and café, the streetscape was always dominated by the imposing frontage of Christ Church Spitalfields opposite the top end of Brushfield Street.

In those days the church was in a shockingly derelict state. Tramps and winos were camped out in its garden and front steps. There was a centre for homeless people in the crypt. The nearby seedy streets, reputedly commanded by Maltese gangsters, were rife with drugs and prostitution. I would not have visited the nearby Jack the Ripper public house, although William Taylor did.

A change of job removed me to Fenchurch Street in 1988. I still visited or passed through the Spitalfields district quite often, but its transformation during the 1990s was not observed by me at detailed first hand. Today, the old fruit and vegetable market is long gone – demolished and replaced by offices, trendy bars and an indoor market hall. Christ Church and its adjoining area are now largely cleaned up.

I would feel safe now to drink at the Jack the Ripper pub, except that it is no longer called that, after a feminist pressure group successfully protested that the old name inappropriately glorified a serial-killer of women. Other residents and sympathisers had also expressed unease about Jack the Ripper being allowed to cast such a prominent cloud over the history and reputation of the district. I doubt that he will ever be obliterated. He remains an enduringly popular tourist attraction, with guided walks regularly crowding the local pavements.

There is a steady stream of interested subscribers too for guided walks through the broader East End, visiting landmarks of its violent political history involving Bolshevik and Fascist activity in the first half of the twentieth-century. During my time of working in the City of London the most frightening street violence associated with the Brick Lane, Spitalfields and Whitechapel area was undoubtedly the era of the 1970s and 1980s. Skinheads went on the march and there was relentless racial intimidation of black immigrants who were taking root in the area.

Towards the end of the 1970s the National Front set up its London headquarters in a building very near to the one where I worked in Great Eastern Street. Sometimes when we returned to work on Monday mornings the police or local council workers would be clearing away debris from a demonstration or some other fracas that had evidently taken place during our absence. A few months later we moved away, rather gratefully, to a new building on the edge of Spitalfields market.

'The Night Watch' – Sarah Waters;
'Hawksmoor' – Peter Ackroyd

Charles Dickens and Sherlock Holmes come first to mind when I try to think of fiction books that are set in the City of London. There are many other books too, but the best one that I have read in recent time, set in the City of London, is by Sarah Waters – 'The Night Watch' (Virago, 2006). The story is set in wartime London. The depiction of life in bomb-strewn London is intensely realistic and was obviously very thoroughly researched by the author.

For me the most powerful narrative sequence in 'The Night Watch' is a late evening walk by Helen and Julia in the City of London. Readers of my generation will have little if any experience of walking through the streets of a big city in pitch darkness, assisted only by weak torchlight. This of course was the norm in 1944 when air raids were still prevalent in London and the black-out remained strictly in force.

Groping their way through the blackness, occasionally bumping into other walkers, Helen and Julia lose their bearings at one point. They think they have arrived at St Clement, in Eastcheap, but they realise that they are on Lombard Street instead and the church they are peering at is St Edmund. The underground stations of Bank and Monument are then passed on their journey, and they are nearly persuaded to dodge into the safety of one of them after they hear the whoosh of a falling bomb, followed by an almighty crash – possibly in nearby Liverpool Street or Moorgate, they estimate from the direction of the noise.

After they reach their intended destination of St Dunstan-in-the-East, in Idol Lane near Tower Hill, the girls stop for a sit-down and a chat. Dotted around the City of London there are quite a few railed-off gardens and squares that are popular places for office workers to sit and eat their sandwiches or read a book. The churchyard of St Dunstan is one such haven of peace: it is situated barely a stone's throw from three different office buildings in which I have worked. St Dunstan was bombed out in wartime and was never rebuilt. Only its Wren tower remains intact. The church's hollowed-out former interior has been neatly landscaped into a garden. The storyline of 'The Night Watch' was resonating so strongly in my mind when I walked round St Dunstan a week after reading the book that I toyed with the idea of commissioning a plaque to be nailed to the door of the church tower: "This is where Helen and Julia walked hand-in-hand, shared a bottle of wine and stole a kiss during an air-raid one night in 1944."

But then I thought: Oh come on Jerry, don't be silly, it was only a story!

Only a story? – well, yes, but as I have earlier mentioned, some authors have included a mixture of fiction and fact in their books about London. Do we always truly know which is which? A trademark of the acclaimed author Peter Ackroyd is to choose London as a theme or background, fusing historical fact with his own invented fiction. In his luminous and beguiling 'Hawksmoor' (Hamilton, 1985) we journey not only between places – Spitalfields and Limehouse – but between different centuries where events and characters seem to juxtapose.

Ackroyd believes that time does not always take a strictly linear path. If this is so, is it possible that before I actually retired from my job, in February 2013, were there days when I walked out of my office for a lunch-hour stroll and I spotted myself across the road, rucksack on my back, walking with a group of "third-agers" enjoying myself looking at churchyards, wall plaques and sundry hidden haunts? Normally there is never enough time to investigate such things during a City worker's ordinary day. So was I getting ahead of myself in my eager anticipation of the day when I would become retired and I could walk all over the City whenever I wanted? Peter Ackroyd would have me believe that this really might have happened!

BROWSING THE ST BOTOLPHS

The pleasant churchyard of St Botolph in Bishopsgate is a much-favoured spot for City workers to sunbathe and picnic during the lunch hour. Architecturally, the most pleasing attraction is the red-brick hall (dating from 1840), though some visitors would probably consider the girls' netball court to outstrip it, if you'll pardon the expression.

One big change that I have noticed in the City during the last twenty years is the growing proliferation of new hotels and restaurants in the area. Right up till the end of the 1980s, a taxi-ride to the West End was almost obligatory if you wanted to take clients out to dinner after work, for there was hardly anywhere you could go in the City.

One of the very few exceptions to this was the former Turkish restaurant at St Botolph near Old Broad Street. Somewhat resembling a submarine in dry-dock, this curiously-shaped building was an oasis in the City's culinary desert. Alas, I never went there. If I had, I might have tested the advice from Jack Burnip, my history teacher at school: "Boys – never, ever, stir Turkish coffee. If you do, the bits all come up to the top, and it will taste disgusting."

I have always considered that St Botolph in Aldgate has one of the most attractive exteriors of any church in the City of London. Have you noticed that the circle-shaped "portholes" in the spire of St Botolph are see-through? Unless you should happen to be carrying a 300-foot high periscope, this charming and unusual feature of a church spire is not evident from street level, although it can be observed if you view the church from a distant vantage-point such as the East India Arms two-thirds of the way along Fenchurch Street.

Walking groups tend to stop outside St Botolph to inspect the drinking fountain, whose inscription to the famous David

Frederick Moccatta (businessman and philanthropist) is one of the few surviving reminders of Jewish influence in the area. It is probably just as well for tourists that I am usually in a big hurry whenever I cross the road at Aldgate and I rush past St Botolph; otherwise I would likely butt in and say: "Do you know that Daniel Defoe was married in this church, in 1683?" This is one of numerous bits of useless information that I have somehow absorbed while working in the City.

St Botolph Aldgate, with the Swiss Re building ("The Gherkin") standing behind.

Another thing that I once noticed about St Botolph was that Ray Buckton, retired leader of the railway drivers union ASLEF, was to be a guest speaker there. This was some twenty years ago. St Botolph Aldgate seems always to live or to have lived on the edge, politically: it champions minority causes and it radiates much more "East End" than "City". I couldn't help pondering that a lynch-mob of City commuters would have stormed into St Botolph if the vicar had dared to give Ray Buckton a platform (sorry) during the 1970s when he and his striking train drivers were Public Enemies Number One of London's working population. My father would throttle me for what I am going to say next, but in hindsight I see Buckton as a hero; so too his peers such as Jack Dash (Dockers Union) and Ted Hill (General Secretary of the United Society of Boilermakers and Iron and Steel Shipbuilders; short name, long name!). If nothing else, these men were orators: if anyone wonders why the City once needed to have nearly one hundred churches within its walls – of which nearly forty are still standing today – I feel sure that simply to step into the pulpit of St Botolph would empower a speaker with a spirit of oratory that would show how and why it is that City of London churches with their old customs and history are different from churches that you find anywhere else in the world.

LOMBARD STREET

I used to walk through Lombard Street nearly every day, going to or from my office. Indeed, one of the insurance companies that I once worked for had the grand name of the Lombard Elizabethan. A "Lombard" was a banker or a moneylender. Seemingly, the word has an Italian association, for Brewer's Dictionary of Phrase & Fable states that in medieval times, Lombard Street in London "became the home of Lombards and other Italian merchants. From the thirteenth century they flourished as pawnbrokers and the three golden balls of the pawnshop are said to be taken from the armorial bearings of the Medici of Florence."

Lombard Street is abundant with historical hallmarks that the present-day pedestrian can easily spot. If you enter the street from Bank tube station you can't miss Hawksmoor's elegant semicircular forecourt and railings at St Mary Woolnoth church. Further up the street is the church of St Edmund, King and Martyr, much restored from Wren's original creation in Portland stone. By the time that you get there you will have passed wall-plaques that commemorate the Post Office and Edward Lloyd's coffee house, while overhead you will have seen ornate gilded signs (cat & cello, grasshopper) that speak of merchants past. You'll have noted too that Change Alley is a street name that reflects the moneylending that has been conducted in and around Lombard Street throughout the centuries.

Brewer's Dictionary is an invaluable aide-memoire that I often consult. I fancy myself to be quite a Chaucer buff but even so I have needed Brewer's to inform me that the Shipman's Tale mentions the merchant who "payd in Parys to certain Lombardes the summe of gold, and hadde of hem his bond."

In his guide book 'City of London Churches' Sir John Betjeman our former poet laureate gives us some grammatical variations: he records of St Michael in nearby Cornhill the presence of a "Lombardised pulpit"; he concludes that alterations by Sir George

Gilbert Scott "tried to make Wren's Classic church Gothic and Lombardic."

"All Lombard Street to a China orange". Mr Evans, the editor confesses to having discarded some old and obscure entries from the 1989 edition of Brewer's Dictionary that I possess. But thank goodness he allowed this delightfully creaky old phrase to escape the cull. I first saw it in a newspaper cutting of 1930, a report of a football match. After scratching my head I deduced that the phrase presumably means overwhelmingly long odds. Brewer bears this out: "To stake the wealth of London against an orange is to stake great wealth against a trifle." The quotation comes from 'The Caxtons' by one Edward George Bulwer Lytton (Baron Lytton) an author who lived from 1803 to 1873.

I suspect that I might be greeted by stares of blank incomprehension if I come out with the expression "All Lombard Street to a China orange". I must try it one day. But long may the phrase survive in the Brewer's Dictionary. I fear alas that a future editor will be forced to push it aside, to make room for the Noughties (the first decade of the twenty-first century) and to insert the likes of "snail mail", "spam" and "spin".

CHEAPSIDE

"The maddest place in all England is Cheapside." So said the essayist Holbrook Jackson, writing in the early 1900s. Cheapside is one of the most important and historic streets in the City of London, but HJ didn't like it. He called it "a monstrous huddle of noisome traffic" and "a roaring canyon of commerce." As soon as he decently could, he slipped away towards Holborn Bars to find his favourite resting place in the quadrangle of Staple Inn.

I can imagine how a foreign visitor to Cheapside might find it mad. Do you know about trying to explain cricket to a foreigner? – "Each man in the side that's in goes out, and when he's out he comes in and the next man goes in till he's out" - etc. Well, how about trying to explain to a foreign visitor that a Londoner is a cockney if he is born within the sound of Bow Bells? While you are pointing out the applicable church of St Mary-Le-Bow, halfway along Cheapside, a number 8 bus sails past, showing Bow Church as its destination. But it is going to Stratford! And if that isn't confusing enough, take your visitor to the opposite side of Cheapside, point out The Guildhall, and say that the Lord Mayor of London is there. "Ah! Boris Johnson!" the visitor will exclaim. "Erm – well, no, actually ..."

I associate Cheapside primarily with pageantry. Each year at the Lord Mayor's Show the City of London dons its coat of many colours and puts on a magnificent display. I have seen imaginative and convincing efforts to display City professions such as insurance on the decorated floats that give colour and life to the procession. The courtyard of The Guildhall is a hub for the annual City Arts Festival and there is a splendid art gallery and reference library. If you like to attend music recitals during weekday lunch hours you are spoilt for choice if you find St Anne & St Agnes, St Lawrence Jewry and St Margaret Lothbury in parallel streets to the east of Cheapside. The big churches St Mary-Le-Bow and St Paul's Cathedral dominate the Cheapside skyline, but please don't ignore St Vedast, tucked away in Foster

Lane: less is more, sometimes, and this charming little church has a subtle serenity. John Betjeman was a warden there.

Historians will tell you what Cheapside has lost: a storm in the year 1090 did away with the original roof of St Mary-Le-Bow, and an anti-Papist riot in 1643 brought the tearing down of an Eleanor Cross like the one that survives outside Charing Cross railway station. But if you wander up and down Cheapside there is plenty of rewarding architecture and history to see. You can breathe in the legend of Dick Whittington who heard the Bow Bells chime "Turn Again Whittington" as he was trudging away towards Highgate. And the fabled giants Gog and Magog are at the Guildhall in effigy, to protect you.

At the old Chepe market in medieval times I daresay that the din was awful, and so too the bustle of the crowds and the handcarts, but did Cheapside really deserve Holbrook Jackson's high scorn in the early 1900s? HJ recorded that he met a friend there, at the corner of Gutter Lane: I thought at first that HJ had deliberately made up this name, to emphasise his hatred of "the roar of the street and the bickering at the Stock Exchange", but no! – a gap in my knowledge of the City was revealed: I have checked the map and there is indeed, off Cheapside, a Gutter Lane! After hearing HJ moan about busy Cheapside symbolising "the discord of modern life in our strident age" his friend made the rejoinder: "It will be a sad day for England when there is no noise in Cheapside."

FISH STREET HILL

I am old enough to remember when you could see for miles from the top of the Monument in the City of London. It was designed by Sir Christopher Wren in the 1670s, to mark where the Great Fire of London started in 1666. I recall my parents taking me there when I was a child, and what a long climb it was to the top: 311 stairs, winding round inside the column.

After I had been at Howdens for a few years we acquired Derek, a new young member of staff whose rather unlikely idea of a fun lunch hour was to stagger all the way up to the top of the Monument and back down again. For the view, it was probably still worth the effort in the early 1970s, but relentlessly since then, more and more high-rise buildings have filled the skyline within the near, medium and far distance range of the Monument's viewing balcony. History tells us that the first challenge came in the 1860s when the commercial prosperity and rising land values of the City of London gathered pace to such an extent that there was an easing of restriction on building heights. After that, the Monument and also many church steeples became obscured by Victorian and Edwardian office blocks. In 1925 there was a direct assault on the Monument when Adelaide House was built next door – an "insolent neo-Egyptian bulk" according to Betjeman. In its opulence it even had a putting-green on its roof.

Today, as you walk across London Bridge looking north, you can only see the burnished flame of the Monument peeping over the top of Adelaide House. In fact there is no perspective, now, from any direction, in which the Monument can be fully seen, save for the close-up views afforded from Fish Street Hill, Gracechurch Street and Monument Street. It is hemmed in on all sides. The nearby Walrus & Carpenter pub is a diverting shrine to Lewis Carroll: the staircase and dining room are adorned with framed drawings from the Alice stories. Not many of the nearby buildings in Lower Thames Street excite me, although I would preserve the attractive Old Billingsgate Hall with its river-facing canopy. Its frontage reminds me of the Liverpool Pier building in the 'Yellow Submarine' film where Ringo races round inside, in a car that changes colour when George drives it. As door after door flies open in the arcade to reveal numerous surreal goings-on, there are some great lines (scripted by Roger McGough): as when Ringo sees Frankenstein inside a museum: "I used to go out with his sister, Phyllis."

Perhaps the greater crime of the building development that has surrounded and hidden the Monument is the near-suffocation too of Wren's magnificent church St Magnus the Martyr. It can now be viewed only from the narrow focus of Fish Street Hill looking down, or in wider but unappealing focus from Lower Thames Street. Its steeple, alas, is invisible from any other direction and only the tip of its gilded vane can be spied from the south side of the Thames or from London Bridge as you cross towards the north. The only saving grace is that even if the builders and planners can stop you seeing St Magnus the Martyr, thank goodness they can't stop you hearing it. I'll warrant that one of the greatest pleasures to be experienced while visiting the City of London is to hear the bells of St Magnus ringing out, as you stand on or above the Thames waterfront by London Bridge.

Beguilingly, a pub sign in Fish Street Hill depicts the Monument with the dome of St Paul's Cathedral shaded in behind. Alas, this is inaccurate, for these two Wren-inspired icons of the City of London skyline are no longer visibly connected. There are too many buildings in the way.

So here's a thought: rather than allow the Monument to be hidden behind bigger, but in another sense lesser structures, why not move the Monument to somewhere more visible? There is precedent for this. When a big stone clock tower became inconvenient in 1867 at its site in the middle of the road approaching London Bridge from the south, it was removed to the seafront at Swanage in Dorset (although they never got round to taking the clock, or supplying another one). Much more recently, at Great Eastern Street where I worked in the late 1970s, a granite obelisk celebrating the Water Board has been re-sited on the pavement next to the Old Fire Station, to allow for a new one-way road traffic system.

Let's even go one step further: let's re-site the church of St Magnus so that its magnificence can be properly appreciated by everyone! If that sounds like a loopy idea, consider this: St Mary Aldermanbury church was removed to Missouri, USA in the 1960s! Even more amazingly the old London Bridge that I first used to cross when I started work in 1966 is now standing in the Arizona desert, and a brand new London Bridge has replaced it! I can well remember watching this epic feat of de-construction and simultaneous re-construction taking place during my early days of commuting. It is sobering to reflect that we all had such great faith in British engineering in those days, whereas today if such a project were taking place, bearing in mind the embarrassing disaster with the nearby Millennium Bridge linking the Tate to St Paul's, I would give any newly-built bridge a wide berth for a few weeks or months, till I were confident that it wouldn't fall down and take me (a non-swimmer) with it.

Sir Christopher Wren is a Great Man of the City of London: it is my opinion that no stone should be unturned, if you'll pardon the expression, to preserve and celebrate a man of whom Betjeman wrote (in 1974): "His cheerful genius pervades the City even today ... his churches were light, varied and happy." There were ninety-seven parish churches within the City before the Great Fire in 1666. Wren afterwards rebuilt fifty-one of them. (A new tax on coal provided some of the funding. Our present-day "austerity taxes" are nothing new!).

> Sir Christopher Wren
> Said, "I am going to dine with some men.
> If anyone calls,
> Say I am designing St Paul's."

Fish Street Hill obtains its name from Billingsgate Fish Market that used to operate nearby. I can remember my father taking me to see it (and no doubt smell it). The market moved away to Docklands in 1982. For many years when I walked through Fish Street Hill on my way to work, it was adorned with a giant street-mural that colourfully and melodramatically depicted the Great Fire. This was eventually dismantled and removed.

A wall-plaque at the Monument informs that King William Street underground station was the very first to serve the City of London, from 1890 to 1900. Nothing now remains of it, whereas the defunct Mark Lane tube station in another part of the City has at least left the useful legacy of a pedestrian subway running beneath the ever-busy Byward Street at Tower Hill. The subway is not prominently signposted: only the initiated are likely to know that it is there: unknowingly, the great flocks of tourists wait and fume at the car-friendly traffic lights that always take ages to turn to red.

AMERICA SQUARE

If you want to find the City of London's best architectural wit, go to America Square. Twenty-odd years ago somebody evidently said: "If it's named after America let's darn well make it look like America." And so the huge edifice of One America Square went swelling into the sky – does it remind me of a giant silver juke-box? – lacking only a Stars & Stripes flag to make complete its conquest of Crosswall.

One America Square has a Mini-Me across the square: America House is one of the buildings that housed the LMCS office that was a central information repository when the Lloyd's and London market was grappling with the three-horned APH (Asbestos, Pollution and Health Hazard) monster in the 1980s and 1990s. I made many visits to that building. In the days before smoking inside offices was banned completely, the LMCS staff had a small room where they were allowed to smoke, and whenever I walked down the corridor and the door to their smoking den happened to be open, it struck me that they might call it the Pollution Room? Incongruities like that have happened to me at other times, too. I remember entering my office building one morning and seeing a tall, attractive if slightly cadaverous lady standing outside, puffing at a cigarette. No – destroying a cigarette would be a better verb, such was the fervency of her inhaling. Later that morning, I saw her being walked round the office and introduced to various managers. "Who's that?" I asked someone. "Oh, she's come to do the Health and Safety inspection."

The feeder roads into America Square resonate with City of London history. Crutched Friars and Minories have religious connotations; part of the City's original Roman wall is displayed between Coopers Row and the Crescent: the latter a small sweep of elegance that was aspired to, perhaps, when America Square was first laid out in 1670. French Ordinary Court and Savage Gardens are two of many curious street names in the City that compel you to consult the reference books: they respectively derive from a long-gone French restaurant where a fixed-price meal was known as an "ordinary", and the seventeenth-century house of Sir Philip Savage. The maritime origins of nearby Pepys Street and Trinity Square are easy to guess.

Staying with my smoking theme it has been said that in the good old bad old days in the Lloyd's and London insurance market there was proverbial "underwriting on the back of a fag packet," a.k.a. "Friday afternoon underwriting" when brokers might secure from underwriters a line on a risk that the underwriter probably wouldn't write when sober on a Monday morning. Did such things truly happen in the 1980s? - I Couldn't Possibly Comment, but approaching America Square on foot from Lloyd's Avenue or under the railway bridge behind Fenchurch Street station I see The Ghosts of Wine Bars Past: for example Marlows, Valentes and above all the Monastery Cellars: a most inappropriate name when one considers what used to go on there: allegedly, I mean, of course.

Poor old Vine Street must have been last in line when they were dishing out interesting and appealing architecture for pedestrians to look at. Someone seems to have taken pity on Vine Street's drabness and has planted on the pavement a multi-coloured tubular structure that looks as though it really belongs in a children's playground. As a Bowring employee in the 1980s it was my entitlement to dine at the St John's Club in Vine Street if I wanted. Here I would likely encounter fellow diners whom taxi-driver Maurice Levinson described as young men from public school who have flats in the West End; he knew that in their own insouciant language they don't take a girl out in the evenings: they "escort" her; and most observantly he noted that they never walk: they always saunter.

The City of London: Wandering and Wondering

FAIR MAIDENS: You can find the Mercers Maiden (top left) near Gracechurch Street. She is more than 300 years old: let me now show you some modern Fair Maidens from the City of London!

HOLBORN AND BLACKFRIARS

As a City of London commuter I came to think of Holborn and Blackfriars as my "back door" way of travelling to and from the City. Commuting via London Bridge or Cannon Street was usually a much faster and more obviously convenient line for me from Orpington, for those termini were the nearest to where I worked in the Lloyd's insurance market in postal district EC3. But on occasions it was an expedient "Plan B" for me to wend my way on the Holborn and Blackfriars line instead. You may know the old Flanders & Swann song: 'The Slow Train'? It references "Millers Dale, Tideswell, Kirby Muxloe, Mow Cop and Scholar Green …" Passengers on the Holborn and Blackfriars line would re-word it: "Sydenham Hill, West Dulwich, Herne Hill and Loughborough Junction …"

There was in fact a time from 1972 to 1974 when Blackfriars railway station was my everyday arrival and departure point for work in the City. This was after Nancy and I had bought our very first property, adjacent to St Mary Cray station on the outskirts of the London Borough of Bromley. I can still remember that my hand shook like a jelly when I wrote out our cheque for the deposit on our flat, and I suspect that afterwards finding the money every month to repay the mortgage was the reason why I never paid a fare to use the tube for completing my journey between Blackfriars and my office in Leadenhall Street. I always walked, instead! - and it was a pleasant route that allowed me to eyeball some of the City's most picturesque sights, including the views across the Thames to Southwark and to the Oxo Tower.

Needless to say, if I retrace that fifteen-minute walk today, forty years later, a great deal has changed. The exterior of the old Blackwall Power Station across the Thames looks little different, I admit, but its interior has been transformed into the thriving Tate Modern Art Gallery. Not only that but a brand new bridge takes pedestrians across to it from Queen Victoria Street: a bridge that on its opening day in 2000 wobbled as alarmingly as my cheque-writing pen had done in 1972!

The reconstructed Globe Theatre, erected on the Southwark waterfront in 1997, is another new sight that I wouldn't have seen in 1972. But as Ralph Waldo Emerson wistfully declared, for everything that is gained, something is lost. I was always fond of walking past the Legal & General Insurance building in Bucklersbury near the Mansion House where the excavated remains of a Roman relic, the Mithras Temple, could be viewed. Today the Roman treasures await being unbundled from the fenced-off big new Bloomberg building development – although as a temporary holding operation until completion of the building in 2016 the developers have most kindly worked with the Museum of London Archaeology to put a colourful and informative display of photographs on the fence for passers-by to see. The display includes photographs of Roman artefacts from the site, and an artist's reconstruction of the Roman loading bay on the long-lost Walbrook River that flowed past in those days but was later covered over. There is also facsimile of a national newspaper article dated 1954, reminding us of the remarkable sensation that it caused in London when the temple (a pagan place of worship) was first discovered.

Altogether during that very first week in 1954 when those Roman ruins were put on public display in Queen Victoria Street more than 100,000 people queued to see them. Hmm - if a new site like that were unearthed nowadays, would there be such mass interest from the populace? My friend Michael Meekums of the Orpington & District Archaeological Society is convinced that there would be. I hope that he is right, for I always found it rather moving, while I was working in the City, to think that near the very spot where I was poring over an insurance file in my office, a Roman stone mason might once have been busy chiselling a stone relief depicting Mithras (the Sun God) slaying a bull, or Roman scribes were busily recording that *Londinium* should henceforth be named *Augusta*, as indeed it was for part of the third century AD.

Seizing on that theme of gain and loss may I briefly reference another of my City heroes? – the late Patrick Hutber. I don't know if you have heard of 'Hutber's Law'? – it was in the 1970s that Mr Hutber, a financial journalist, coined 'Hutber's Law' in advancement of his theory that whenever the government, or any of the service companies (for example: a bank or a utility company) or the people who run the organisation that you work for announce a new change of system or procedure and proclaim that it will be an "improvement" you can usually bet that in practice it will prove to be anything but!

In his own lifetime, sadly curtailed by a fatal motor accident, Patrick Hutber cited several examples of a so-called improvement that either cunningly or unintentionally hid what was really deterioration. Now if you have worked in an office, same as I and many thousands of other clerks or managers have done in the Lloyd's and London insurance market you'll likely have encountered the universal 'Murphy's Law' (what can go wrong, will go wrong) and possibly too the 'Peter Principle' (people will be promoted to their level of incompetence). And don't forget 'Parkinson's Law: The Pursuit of Progress' in which the wry Cecil Northcote Parkinson advocated in 1958 his theory that work always expands to fill the time of the number of staff that are employed to do it. Superb cartoons by Osbert Lancaster make 'Parkinson's Law' an all-time classic work of satire on office life and human nature. Mr Parkinson worked in the Civil Service where, of repute, everything has to be done in triplicate and the hierarchy of authorisation is greatly bloated: we in the London insurance market may fancy that we are much too sharp and commercial to carry any inefficiencies in our organisations, but if you ask me to swear on the Bible that during my forty-six years at Lloyd's there was never a time when I saw 'Parkinson's Law' in operation I would be temporarily struck silent!

Although my visits to the west of the City districts of Holborn and Blackfriars became rather sporadic after 1974 there was always plenty for me to see, learn and enjoy when I did go there.

My weakness for interesting and unusual road names in the City is amply fulfilled in Holborn by the likes of Old Seacoal Lane, Saffron Hill and Snow Hill. Meanwhile, anyone with a foot fetish would surely like Hosier Lane, Leather Lane and Shoe Lane? Staying with that last one, the letter 'S' also conjures up the Shoe Lane Library that is sunken into the subterranean strata. There is also the thought of the amusing 'School Dinners' restaurant. It opened near Holborn Viaduct in the 1970s and was one of the first enterprises to encourage City businessmen to switch off their supposed stresses and strains and enjoy a lunch hour or evening of being supremely silly, instead.

Architecturally there is a small stretch of High Holborn that offers one of the City's most dramatic contrasts of period. The black and white timber frame frontage of Staple Inn leans out over the pavement: it is one of very few wooden buildings that can still be found in London. Its striking façade is a twentieth-century restoration, but according to the experts it looks like a faithful replica of the Elizabethan original.

Close by, two giant insurance companies beginning with the letter 'P' have weighed in with heavyweight architectural pieces of their own. Situated diagonally opposite Staple Inn, the Prudential Assurance building seems to be very unlike its name, given its outrageous flame-red brick and its aggressive Gothic combination of arches, gables and roof-spike. And then further along from Staple Inn can be encountered the Pearl Assurance building, a fussy Edwardian neo-Baroque extravaganza topped off by a structure that looks a little too self-important to be called a cupola but not quite the Full Monty to qualify as a dome?

Neither the Pearl nor the Prudential building continues to be occupied or used by its founders. Pearl moved out in 1990 and the marble floors, columns and tiling of its former headquarters serve nowadays for delight and delectation of guests and visiting diners at the upmarket Chancery Court Hotel. The Prudential is now a multi-occupied building whose resplendent interior courtyard (Waterhouse Court) boasts some fine terracotta and - above a wide arch - rows of imitation Tudor windows that suggest themselves to my suspicious mind as possibly being a cheeky attempt to steal the thunder of the nearby Staple Inn as oldest-looking building on the block?

(By the way, if you think that I might be over-reacting to call a flame-red City building "outrageous" do please remember that the author PG Wodehouse once had Bertie Wooster declare that with girls of high and haughty spirit one must always be careful lest they fly off the handle, especially if they have red hair.)

The row of shops at Staple Inn was pictured in yesteryear on tins of 'Old Holborn' tobacco. I don't know whether a Queen Bess's Ye Olde Tea Shoppe has ever traded there, or might do so one day in the future, but at the very least, it seems to me that minstrels should always be there, playing the viol and the lute! That said, a few yards further along High Holborn, the ornate red-brick Staple Inn Building glories today in the business name of The Glamour House! Now to my mind Holborn is a district of the City that can proudly puff out its chest and brag about its history. It is sited on the original Roman road from London to Colchester, and in addition to remaining an important commercial thoroughfare it became in its own right a centre of excellence for small trades and industries: evidence for this was the enormous count of pubs and taverns to be found there! Holborn was referenced by King Edgar in AD 959; one William Fitzstephen (1154 – 1189) recorded that its open lands were popular for sporting activities such as archery, javelin-throwing, wrestling and, er, football; the Knights Templar set up a base there; Lincoln's Inn and Staple Inn and other Inns of Court would also find homes there. Charles Dickens set two of his novels there; the author Rachel Lichtenstein has just published her excellent new book 'Diamond Street' (2012) that lifts the lid on the fascinating history of Hatton Garden and the secretive community of jewellery traders that operated there.

But if I interrogate Holborn about its present-day complexion, can it convince me that it is nowadays glamorous? Take some of the statues, for example. Prince Albert (on horseback) merrily doffs his hat and radiates *joie de vivre* - or in his case should I say *lebensfreude*. But his is one of those exasperating statues that are difficult to photograph satisfactorily. It doesn't matter which angle you try, the faded black-stained-green colour of the statue doesn't show up well against any of the rather uninspiring array of modern buildings that stand on the corners of the six main roads that converge at Holborn Circus.

A best try, perhaps, is to use as background the off-white Portland stone tower of St Andrew Holborn: but there's a vexing little let-down here too. From a distance, the Charity boy and girl figures on the exterior church wall look rather sweet in their respective blue coat and frock, trimmed with white. From close-up, unfortunately, they look as though a lick of paint wouldn't go amiss. St Andrew is one of the City's biggest and grandest churches: its history involves Wren, Handel, World War Two bombing and restoration: I hesitate to groan about some temporary chipped paintwork there, especially as one of my friends might likely suggest to me that now I am retired from work haven't I got the time to hire a van, buy a stepladder and some paint from Wilko and go and spruce things up myself!

The war memorial to the Royal Fusiliers in High Holborn is another that loses detail against its background: the exterior grey stone of the London School of Business has an unfortunate camouflaging effect on the statue of the soldier, although the onlooker can certainly read the inscription that tells of 22,000 men lost in World War One, and more in World War Two. There is a pretty Garden of Remembrance for the Royal Fusiliers at the church of St Sepulchre Without Newgate, near to Holborn Viaduct and known as the Musicians' Church.

I pass one of my favourite City of London statues when I'm walking up Fetter Lane towards Holborn Circus. When I say that I pass it I must confess that I always feel a faint if irrational urge to hurry past the awe-inspiring effigy of the fearsome parliamentarian and radical John Wilkes (1725 – 1797) lest he should break off from the manifesto that he is reading and buttonhole me for a stern lecture about freedom and reform.

If on the whole I favour Blackfriars over Holborn for aesthetic quality of buildings, monuments and landscape it's probably for the unfair reason that Blackfriars has the Thames, and the views that go with it, while Holborn is now in dry dock after the old Fleet River was long ago covered over and dispensed with as a commercial asset to the district. Its demise was sealed in 1733: traders gave up on it as a cargo route because of irregular flow of water, silting by Thames mud, and clogged-up sewage.

St Bride's church with its distinctive "wedding cake" spire is a special jewel of the Blackfriars district. It is another Wren masterpiece. I can commend too the Bridewell Theatre that stages some lively fringe productions within the portals of the St Bride's Institute where I used to play competitive chess in the London League after first coming up to the City.

In summary: commuting to work by rail has been the biggest single factor that has given me cause to make occasional walks to and from Blackfriars and Holborn. If trains haven't been running on the London Bridge line or have experienced big delays it has been second nature for me to divert myself over to Blackfriars or Holborn instead.

On that note, I must finish by paying tribute to the young man (well, I have never met him, but he sounds young) whose public announcements over the tannoy at Bank underground tube station are of utmost merit. "Ladies and gentlemen, there is a good service operating today on all lines!" – and he says it with such a calming, soothing assurance that it sounds to be plausible and true! Not only do I feel imbued with a sudden uplifting sense of optimism: this young man sounds so much in command of things and so unruffled that I really wonder if I should consult him for advice on my stock market holdings, and ask him too if he can think of a cure for my habit of embarking on a little walk around the City that often ends up being a much longer walk, because I become so enthralled by all the interesting things that there are to see!

OLD FATHER THAMES

The River Thames is integral to the City of London's landscape. One of the best things that has happened during my forty-six years of commuting is the various London authorities combining to give pedestrians a continuous Thames-side walk. To cite just one example, within the last fifteen years the south bank alongside Tooley Street has been paved and lawned, so that you can amble along and look across to the City, while passing such tourist attractions as Hays Galleria, the HMS Belfast and even Southwark Crown Court where some of the City's less scrupulous financiers have found themselves to be unwilling visitors.

My friend Janet Crotty was duly encouraged to take me on occasional route-marches in the lunch hour when the sun was shining, and prove to me that we really could get as far as Blackfriars, then loop across to Southwark, and along and back to Ace Insurance by 2pm eager and refreshed to resume our inspection of policy documents. In addition to enjoying our habitual literary discussions Janet and I were arrested by the Clink Prison - not literally! and by the ever-increasing number of similar historical-interest items that have recently been added along the route, such as the attractive new displays inside the foot-tunnel that connects Tower Hill to St Katherine's Dock, the glazed tiles in the tunnel at Blackfriars showing images of the architects' and engineers' drawings for the bridge, and the engraved paving stones depicting medieval riverside scenes inside the brick tunnel beneath Southwark Bridge.

Robert Philpotts is author of two excellent little booklets 'On Foot in the East End' published in the early 1990s. These walking-guides were an invaluable boon to me while I briefly worked outside the City in Docklands and I made car journeys along The Highway from Tower Hill past Wapping, then along Narrow Street (aptly named: nose-to-tail traffic jams until they opened the Limehouse Tunnel). As pointed out by Mr Philpotts that journey would have taken me past orchards and grazing sheep, in bygone days before the Industrial Revolution. After thumbing through his books to find intriguing references to the 'Bow Cemetery Grieving Committee' (1890s) and 'Pudding Mill Lane' I was hooked on wanting to find out everything that I could about my new surroundings. I never quite got round to the recommended walk from Mile End to Three Mills with enticing opportunity to see the Northern Outfall Sewer, but I did like reading about 'Channelsea' – a series of creeks and channels on the River Lea: names such as this, and 'Queenhithe' – the old City harbour at London Bridge – exert great enjoyment upon me.

I struggle to remember exactly how busy the Thames was, as a port clogged with ships and cranes unloading at the wharves, when I first started work in the City of London in 1966. In the last two or three decades the riverfront has undergone an extraordinary transformation, such that it is lined now with converted or new-built apartment blocks and offices where I would only have seen derelict and rat-infested wharves standing in the 1970s. Today though, if you want to nose them out, there are still a few nooks and crannies such as Shad Basin and Spice Wharf in north Bermondsey that hold some atmosphere from the past.

A clue is offered by the film 'Georgy Girl' (1966). The young lovers – Alan Bates and Lynn Redgrave – take a boat trip down the Thames, passing St Paul's Cathedral (its dome covered by a curious white cowl – scaffolding, I presume) and on towards Tower Bridge and Wapping. There is evidence enough in the background landscape to show that the Pool of London was still in operation, albeit on a fast-reducing scale because everything was moving downstream to deepwater ports such as Tilbury where the new big container ships could dock and unload.

My friend and neighbour the late Donald Ward worked at the Post Office in Aldersgate, near St Paul's, after the war. He was a published poet. On a Thames theme, I love his poem 'Southwark Cathedral' that begins: "Trains cross its roofs." Later in the poem we get: "Porters unload oranges and oaths … The warehouse dangles its chains."

I fancy too that Donald was walking across London Bridge one night, perhaps after working the late shift, and he gazed down into the water and afterwards began his poem 'The Bridge':

> Night leans upon the wharves;
> The straight cranes
> Crash in the water, weave and dance
> Tumbling and waving their atrophied limbs
> Into bizarre forms and images.
> All structure melts, all buildings limp away …

St Katherine's Dock is a self-contained waterside sanctuary to the north of Tower Bridge. Was the tourist trap that is the Dickens Inn especially in the spotlight in 2012? – not only visitor volumes being swelled by the Olympic Games but the 200th anniversary of the birth of Charles Dickens. Thomas Telford built St Katherine's Dock in the early 1800s, for the principal purpose of providing an enclosed and walled area to make cargoes safer from an alarming epidemic of pilfering in the London Docks. (Is there a Telford around today to build something to stop metal cables being pinched from our railway tracks?). Long-ago trade from faraway is commemorated at West Dock where model elephants adorn the gateposts; Ivory House, built in 1854, is now a complex of modern offices and shops.

The artist Rachel Whiteread, a resident of the City of London, has said: "The Thames is a great, great asset. I love cycling along the Thames Path on the south side, or going along the canals up to the Olympic site." My favourite of her works was her famous or infamous life-size cast 'House' that I would see in the early 1990s on nights when I chose to drive home from work through Bow and the Blackwall Tunnel. I could never understand why there was such a fuss about the 'House' and why the authorities were in such a tearing hurry to remove it. Well, at least Rachel was commissioned to decorate the exterior of the Whitechapel Art Gallery with a frieze to celebrate the Olympic Games taking place in London in 2012, and her resultant laurel of golden leaves is a welcome permanent addition to outdoor art in the City

The Thames to the east of the City of London is entrancing to me. If I take my childhood love of my clockwork train-set, and marry this to my being a water-sign (Scorpio) this might explain why I always look forward to a ride on the Docklands Light Railway. If I choose a bright day when the sky is clear blue, and the sun is flecking the water surfaces of the many waterways and pools that the train passes on its journey, or alternatively if the wind is still and the water is clear and limpid, I don't think that London can offer anything more visually satisfying and spectacular than a ride on the DLR.

As the train noses out of Lewisham with the River Quaggy running alongside, one quickly encounters Rachel Whiteread's "amazing juxtaposition of the old and the new" as the jazzy and colourful new-build flats and studios at Deptford Bridge preface the Greenwich Basin lined with dark-bricked nineteenth-century industrial works. After that, the train burrows beneath the Thames to emerge in the Isle of Dogs. (THE NEXT STOP IS ISLAND GARDENS! THE NEXT STOP IS MUDCHUTE! etc).

The landscape of the Isle of Dogs was transformed with astonishing rapidity after the London Docklands Development Corporation was founded in 1981. It took less than five years for the dock area to become altered beyond recognition. Major drainage work to facilitate the construction of the DLR was followed by the building of new commercial offices, while around the river's edge, old factory sites and wharves were swept away to make space for expensive new private apartments and housing estates.

That new landscape comes excitingly alive as the DLR train swooshes and bleeps its way from South Quay to Westferry, passing beneath the soaring skyscrapers and linkways of the Canary Wharf business park. Docklands as "Second City" (or even "First City") has its disbelievers, but if you ride through on a Monday to Friday during commercial hours it makes the most powerful impact to see the vast rows and rows of battery-hen workers seated in front of their flickering flat-screens. Shades, surely, of the folk-singer Pete Seeger and his song 'Little Boxes' that was often heard on the radio when I was a child.

At Westferry you can change trains and let the DLR show you the eastward extent of this magical JG Ballard 'Super-Cannes': the London City Airport, the new Billingsgate Fish Market, the Excel Centre, the site of the Olympic Games at Stratford. Otherwise, stay on the train as it arrows you towards the City of London, terminating at Bank or Tower Gateway. On this stretch of the line, passing through Limehouse, you'll see some eye-catching new-build apartments on the waterfronts, but the prevailing vista is distinctly East End council. The worst slums have gone, but you can easily imagine scenes of Victorian and early twentieth-century poverty and hard labour among the present-day tenement blocks, where names such as Coburg Dwellings evoke a Joseph Conrad world of eastern European immigrants and anarchists. On the outside at least, some of the old tenement blocks such as Moore House and Vogler House have been spruced up to look neat and colourful – faintly Art Deco, even – were they given priority for a facelift, for the benefit of spectators on the DLR?

Tower Bridge is a perennial tourist attraction and I don't doubt that its Victorian mechanisms are praiseworthy; but I am surely not the only pedestrian or motorist who has been irritated to be held waiting – me and many thousand others – while the bridge goes up to allow a few Hooray Henrys on a tall-masted pleasure-boat to sail beneath. It seems disproportionate? The one and only time that I was passing by the Tower of London during the ceremonial firing of cannons for the Queen's Birthday, it astonished me how loud the noise is. As for the tourist option to cross Tower Bridge by the very top walkway, just beneath the two pinnacles, I have no head for heights, so I say no thanks: for me that high-up walk is a "bridge too far"!

A riverboat trip to Greenwich from Tower Pier was a delightful staff excursion and swan-song for the twenty of us from CNA whose sector of the company was sold in 2007. Riverbus services along the Thames have not always been profitable: Mr Philpotts tells us that the passenger steamboat *King William IV* couldn't make money there in the 1830s but was profitably deployed afterwards on long voyages that took emigrants all the way to Australia. So, did we miss a trick in 2007? Should we have hi-jacked the boat and sailed on past Greenwich, out beyond the Thames estuary and on to start a New Life in the New World? I have friends in the London reinsurance market who emigrated to Australia: But could I ever find the Snowy river to be an acceptable replacement for the Thames?

The City of London: Wandering and Wondering

Tower Hill seen from the opposite side of the Thames, next to City Hall, the Mayor of London's new headquarters built in 2002.

King's Cross

NORTH LONDON

When I write of the City of London, I am aware that I carry in my head a mental map of the City that doesn't quite comport with its official boundaries.

"My" City of London stops more or less where it should on three sides: east, south and west. Brick Lane defines my idea of the east: insurance companies in Leman Street (for example, the former JH Minet) just about scrape in! The Thames makes it easy to mark the south, where I deem that the City spans the northern edge that runs along from Tower Bridge, London Bridge and Southwark Bridge. I might allow the Mayor of London's office, Southwark Cathedral and Tooley Street to be included as "City" too, but sooner or later I've got to declare that I'm in Bermondsey or Borough, and that's "out"! Meanwhile to the west I'm aware from my days as an insurance and reinsurance practitioner that I characterise St Paul's to Chancery Lane as bandit country of law firms (and, once upon a time before they all decamped to Docklands and Wapping, newspapers).

It is to the north that I give myself poetic licence – literally! – in deciding what's "City". This maybe started in 1976 when I worked in Great Eastern Street, just along from Old Street, and I found myself at the gateway to arty Islington, enclave of up-and-coming well-to-do City types whose invasion of this former run-down working class borough had sent property prices rocketing skywards. (May I mention, in passing, that when an international chess tournament was held there in the 1970s, the Russians pronounced "Islington" to make the first syllable rhyme with "aisle".)

Having grown up as a child in Mill Hill, postal district NW7 – it is near Barnet, Finchley and Hendon – was I starting to be drawn back there, like a magnet, when chance took me to work in Old Street and I was reconnected to the familiar black stripe of the Northern Line on the tube map? The answer is that for the next few years I happily foraged around the confines of Old Street's unconsidered fringe-of-the-City area, and it wasn't till a later time in my life that I set my cap at the further outposts of Euston and King's Cross (arts, books, family history, films, Housmans Bookshop) and Highgate Hill (art, literature, and Lubetkin's iconic 1930s Art Deco apartment block at High Point).

Old Street with its evocative street names (Curtain Road, Tabernacle Street, Willow Street) and occasional thrilling buildings (Alexandra Trust and the Leysian Mission near the tube station, Courtyard Theatre in Pitfield Street, St John's Church in Hoxton with its fantastic Pre-Raphaelitesque ceiling) was enough to hold my interest in the late 1970s, but maybe bigger seeds were sown. North London is without parallel in our capital city as an area that is populated by actors, artists, beatniks, designers, painters, poets, political activists and writers. Many of them are immigrants – from Europe especially. They span the alphabet from Dannie Abse to Zen Buddhists! – and dotted in my calendar during the last fifteen or so years, I find that I have gravitated towards them, to attend or join in cultural activities and events.

These affiliations of mine in North London can be ephemeral: for example, after I had hooked up with a poetry group at the Torriano Meeting House in Kentish Town, it sadly transpired that in early 2010, the leader John Rety and my main friend in the group Phil Poole both passed away. And, alas, I stopped going after that.

Another little haunt of mine was, and potentially still is, the London Metropolitan Archives. It is hidden away in Clerkenwell – another of north London's fascinating little quarters where there is some eye-catching and surprising architecture to browse. Principally, the LMA is a resource centre for family history research, but it also houses London history lectures.

Now look, I am not trying to purport that the City of London stretches so far north that it straddles a large area of Middlesex; if

I have ventured further north than Archway, I am probably making some sort of subliminal "return to the womb": I note, at any rate, that in any postal district beginning with an 'N' I can always immediately get my bearings; I feel that I have come "home".

Nor does my eulogy of North London match the enthusiasm of a pen friend from my schooldays who took my breath away when she told me what was top of her list of things to see when she and her friend were coming to London. Never mind Big Ben, Buckingham Palace, the Tower of London ... the must-see place for her was "Finchley Central, on the Northern Line" – from the song by the New Vaudeville Band that was a chart hit in 1967.

Roy Hattersley, former Deputy Prime Minister and occasional columnist in our daily newspapers, thinks it's a disgrace that London has no proper statue of Shakespeare: apart from "a crude likeness" in Leicester Square. RH is a big fan: he loves to insist that Shakespeare defines England and Englishness and that he is the man who makes England different from the rest of the world. It is RH's opinion that the world's greatest plays about love, ambition, jealousy and grief have all been written by the Bard.

RH will hopefully be gratified by the news that the Shakespeare statue and fountain in Leicester Square is being upgraded – although I do rather perversely wonder if some tourists will be disappointed when it is eventually unveiled, because the temporary protective cladding has a mirrored surface that is proving very popular for passers-by to photograph themselves in the reflection! I ask too if RH is unaware of the attractive if small statue of Shakespeare that stands in Aldermanbury, EC2? And is it legitimate for me to suggest that it is symbolic that the statue is sited on the City of London's northern edge? - as though to say – to boast, even – that literary North London is the right and natural place for the world's greatest writer to be commemorated?

At the Barbican, the cinema, library and theatre are foremost cultural assets for City of London residents and workers. Beware the dastardly 2pm closing time of the library on Fridays, but celebrate its colourful and informative monthly newsletter; enjoy too the commendable variety of Book Events that are offered at regular intervals: currently (2011 into 2013) a feast of 1930s crime fiction books in which characters with names like Basil say things like: "How the deuce should I know that seedy-looking blighter?"

Great Eastern Street

Shakespeare at Aldermanbury

Another literary statue on the northern edge of the City of London allows me to pay tribute to my late friend Phil Poole. The anniversary of John Milton (1608 – 1674) was celebrated in Britain in November 2008. During an exchange of e-mails with Phil while this was happening, I chanced to tell him that I had not previously realised that Milton was buried at St Giles Cripplegate, in the Barbican.

The next thing I knew, Phil had nipped along to St Giles to take a look for himself, and he had composed a poem that I think is one of the best new poems that I have seen in recent years.

MILTON'S STATUE
(in St Giles, Cripplegate, Barbican where he lies)

In the last night of a December day
you stand dark bronze and you are not yet blind
though you are gone from us who only find
effigy. Speechless yet you may speak to me.

I think you know what Wordsworth said of you –
Virtue, Freedom, Power. An intelligence
above the law exists but makes no sense
if not above men – aye – and women too.
I'll read some of your lines again. Repeat
what was given to you to say here on earth.
"I wak'd, she fled -" O there is little mirth

and yet as day goes I sense a sad smile
in the besieged church, mettle reaching out
freely to help our light. I'll stand awhile.

In an earlier e-mail to me, Phil had referred to WH Davies's well known poetic lines:

> What is this life, if full of care,
> We have no time to stop and stare?

Simple words – but they speak volumes. They express a sentiment that I can only commend to workers in the City of London. In my forty-six years of Mondays to Fridays there, I tried to take time out from the busy office routine, so that I could find, admire and enjoy the numerous interesting things that there are to see and do in the City.

Commuters approaching the City from the north and east can see the post-Olympics regeneration that will gift the capital city the new Queen Elizabeth Olympic Park opening in July 2013.
Photograph Copyright ©2013 Les Cheeseman

AND SO IT CAME TO PASS

Football, and my Freedom Pass

Not long after I joined Howdens in 1966, I turned out for their football team on Saturday afternoons. Howdens was one of the biggest and most prestigious insurance and reinsurance brokers in the London market, but, curiously, instead of playing in the Insurance League, their football club belonged only to the Shipping League. This derived, I was told, from the company's nautical origins in the long and distant past. Opposing teams on our fixture list in 1966 were accordingly drawn from obscure firms of charterers, freight forwarders and shipbrokers that I had never heard of.

Howdens moreover used a football pitch that was not "commensurate with their dignity". (I have borrowed that phrase from the famous football writer Brian Glanville). Not for them one of the luxurious and manicured sports grounds that proliferated in areas of south London such as Beckenham and Dulwich. Instead, they played on a cabbage-patch in North Woolwich, situated next to an evil-looking pub whose clientele – the Saturday ones, anyway – needed only the clock to be rolled back to the year 1790 to look suitable candidates to be shackled and shipped to Botany Bay on the next high tide.

I soon became bored by the long and convoluted journey that I had to make by public transport from my home on Saturday mornings, concluding with a ride on the Woolwich ferry, to reach the Howdens sports ground. What I really liked to do on Saturday afternoons was watch football – my beloved local team Cray Wanderers in particular. A big bonus for me in starting work in London in 1966 was my becoming sufficiently adventurous and capable of using public transport to get myself across London to see the Wanderers play in far-off counties outside Kent. Until that time, I had rarely ventured to away games that were distant from where I lived.

My rapidly-learned knowledge of the London transport network did not rival the expertise of a group of my school friends who attempted in the mid-1960s to break the world record for visiting every single London Underground station in one continuous journey within 24 hours. I cannot recall whether they were successful, but I hope that the authorities were kind enough to grant them a free One-Day Travelcard, or maybe it was called a Red Rover in those days?

My less strenuous "roving" enabled me to enjoy an uninterrupted spell of late 1960s watching of the Wanderers in such diverse places as Harlow, Hillingdon and Hornchurch – or, to use the vernacular of many of my fellow Cray-ites, 'Arlow, 'Illingdon and 'Ornchurch.

I did not know it at the time, but this was all a most useful rehearsal for the later time in my life, in November 2007, when I gained my cherished Freedom Pass. Free travel on London's public transport - on weekdays after 9.30am and at any time during weekends! Goodbye to train fares or to road tax and petrol expenditure! If I wished to travel to the outermost boundaries of the metropolis I could do so for nothing, by bus, tube or train.

Yes, that is the purpose of owning a Freedom Pass. It comes in a pocket-size open-out wallet that is bright red in colour. It was a gift to me on my sixtieth birthday from Red Ken, but since then the Mayor of London has become Bonkers Boris instead. Will Boris demand that the wallets must now be coloured blue? Not that it is mandatory to carry your Freedom Pass in the regulation red wallet. You can buy your own wallet of any colour and slot your Freedom Pass inside it if you wish. Word reaches my ears that quite a few Londoners, mainly of the female gender, have done exactly that, for fear that the ubiquitous red wallet is too visible a giveaway of their true age if anyone sees them at the ticket barrier for the train or bus.

What a wide range of places to visit! To the north-east, Epping Forest; to the south-east, Rainham Marshes in Essex, once improbably touted as the venue for the new EuroDisney until they chose Paris instead! (It opened in 1995). To the north-west, Metro-Land, as immortalised in John Betjeman's television documentary in 1974. And to the south-west, the stockbroker belt of Surrey, also lauded by Betjeman (in poems about Camberley, Coulsdon, Croydon, etc).

When my Cray-watching is facilitated by my new toy the Freedom Pass, I feel an indefinable buzz of excitement when I arrive at Orpington railway station at midday and I join the great throng of people heading up to London for their Saturday afternoon sport or other entertainment. This is something that is missed when journeying by car, as had been my custom for many years. An infectious enthusiasm is engendered by the sight on the station platform of all the replica football shirts, scarves, hats or other apparel identifying that the wearer is on his or her way to watch Arsenal, Charlton, Chelsea, Millwall – or alternatively Harlequins, London Irish or Wasps for those of the oval ball persuasion.

Friendly banter is engaged. "Who are you playing today?" From this one learns that Nick Hornby was spot-on when he described the mental state of every football supporter as one of permanent disgruntlement and anxiety. Question: "How is your team doing lately?" Typical Reply (1): "Absolute crap. The manager hasn't got a clue. I don't know why we keep going every week." Or – Typical Reply (2): "We've won our last two games, but we are not playing well, sooner or later we are going to get a right hammering!"

There are other confessions to make. Despite my many years of Monday to Friday commuting to work, I have never quite lost the smug little tingle that ripples through me when I board a train to London on a Saturday or Sunday knowing that my destination is not going to be the office. I must admit too that I am still a big kid when it comes to taking tube or train rides around the Home Counties. When he wrote his famous poem about the thrill of railway journeys, looking out of the carriage window as the world flashes past, Robert Louis Stevenson certainly spoke for me. Alas though, he spoke for me too on the occasions when the Wanderers have had a run of good results and I am confidently expecting another win. Warning of me the jarring experience that can sometimes lie in wait, Stevenson wrote: "It is sometimes better to travel hopefully than to arrive!"

LONDON BY THE SEA

Swanage Town Hall with façade of the old Mercers Hall in the City of London.

If I were to tell you that there is a place called London by the Sea, would you know what I am talking about?

The place that I mean is the picturesque seaside resort of Swanage, in Dorset. I had better reference the fact that there are two separate local authorities on this: one refers to Swanage as 'Old London by the Sea' and the other to 'Little London by the Sea'. But in both cases it is Swanage that is meant; and the London is for the most part the City of London; and the connecting factor of it all is the quarrying of Purbeck stone.

On a visit to Swanage in 1724, the London-born Daniel Defoe wrote:

"This part of the County is eminent for Vast Quarreys of Stone, which is cut out Flat, and us'd in London in great quantities for Paving Court-Yards, Alleys, Avenues to Houses, Kitchins, Foot-Ways and the like; profitable to the Place, as is also the Number of Shipping employ'd in bringing it to London. There are also several Rocks of very good Marble, only that the Veins in the Stone are not Black and White, as the Italian, but Grey, Red and other Colours."

After the Great Fire of London in 1666 there had been a big call for Purbeck stone to help rebuild the capital city. This was not the first time that it had been used: historians have recorded that in the twelfth and thirteenth centuries the stone trade from the Isle of Purbeck amounted to an enormous tonnage. One of its uses was for the rebuilding of Westminster Abbey in 1245.

The names of John Mowlem (1788 – 1868) and his nephew George Burt (1816 – 1894) are written large in the connecting history between Swanage and the City of London. Mowlem was a successful builder and stone merchant, and Burt later followed him into the stone trade, where he would make his mark as an ambitious entrepreneur and developer.

Not only did these notable gentlemen supply the City of London with material such as paving for Fleet Street and Strand in the 1850s: they also took away discarded items of City of London architecture and transported them to Swanage to enjoy a second life there, by the seafront.

I have already mentioned how the Wellington Clock Tower, being an obstruction to traffic at the Southwark end of London Bridge, ended up in Swanage. It was shipped there in the *Mayflower* in 1867. Moreover if you walk past Swanage Town Hall its striking seventeenth-century stone façade was acquired by John Burt from the old Mercers Hall in Cheapside, when the Town Hall was built in 1882.

Burt had earlier built the imposing Purbeck House in 1875, incorporating cast-iron balustrades and columns taken from the Billingsgate Fish market and also items from the second of the three Royal Exchange buildings – the one that burned down in 1838. Add to that a sprinkling of City of London bollards, cannon posts and lamp standards that have been transplanted in various parts of the town of Swanage and you'll see how its respective nicknames of 'Old London by the Sea' and 'Little London by the

Sea' have come about! One eagle-eyed local historian has noted that one of the bollards – many of them came from Clerkenwell and St Giles – has a mis-spelt inscription "City of Lodno".

John Mowlem is visibly commemorated in Swanage by the large structure of the Mowlem Theatre on the seafront. Next to it stands a stone obelisk with black cannon balls on top: this was built at Mowlem's insistence that the town should remember the brave feat of King Alfred's navy when defeating the Danes in a sea-battle outside Swanage Bay in AD 877. Never mind that some historians dispute that this battle ever happened! – there are times when we surely must allow romance to triumph over fact? Talking of which, the famous Enid Blyton, a prolific and popular author of books for children, was a regular holidaymaker in Swanage and is said to have based many of her fictional 'Famous Five' adventure stories there. When the Five typically find secret caves and tunnels in seaside locations this is very likely an echo of the real-life quarrying industry in Swanage whose history was known to Enid Blyton.

Today in Swanage you can walk up to Durlston Head and although the Tilly Whim Caves (great name!) are nowadays closed to the public because they are too dangerous to enter, you can find on the cliff-top a deliberately-preserved stone quarry with an information board that recounts the everyday hard labouring life of the stoneworkers of old. And if you walk today in the City of London there are places where you can still find some of the work-products that came there, a century or more ago, from those worthy men of Dorset.

ST. OLAVE'S CHURCH

Forward!
Christ - Men
Cross - Men

"OUR OWN CHURCH"

Samuel Pepys

WHO CAME THROUGH THIS GATE FROM THE NAVY OFFICE AND HIS HOME IN SEETHING LANE TO WORSHIP HERE.

"MY BEST BELOVED CHURCHYARD THE CHURCHYARD OF ST GHASTLY GRIM"

Charles Dickens

"THE UNCOMMERCIAL TRAVELLER"

FROM THE BURIAL REGISTER
1586 SEPT. 14TH MOTHER GOOSE
1665 (THE GREAT PLAGUE) 365 Names
1703 JUNE 4TH SAMUEL PEPYS Esq.
Buried in a Vault under Ye Communion Table

The City of London: Wandering and Wondering

Barbican

Snowman on the plaza of the Aviva building in St Mary Axe. In the background, new and old architecture of the Lloyd's building in Leadenhall Street.

Sun Court, Cornhill – and friends from Mottingham Library Reading Group. The new Lloyd's building is visible in the distance.

Roman history at Walbrook

Double street sign at High Holborn

Sean Millwall: "Support Our Troops". A rainy day in London Town.

THE WARD OF LANGBOURN

"London, thou art the flower of cities all!" Cleary Gardens.

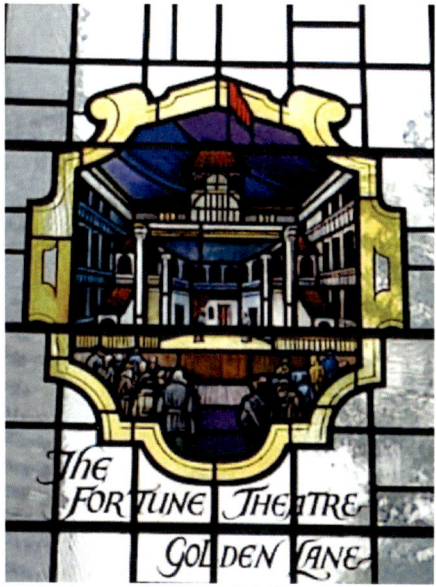

Stained-glass window: St Giles Cripplegate.

Reflection: 100 Leadenhall Street, frontage of the Ace building.

The City of London: Wandering and Wondering

PEOPLE

The Barge Master & Swan Master at Garlick Hill, Ward of Vintry.

GEOFFREY CHAUCER & JOHN BETJEMAN

What must it be like to live in the heart of the City of London? Weird, I have often thought. But the artist Rachel Whiteread evidently doesn't mind: she declared in July 2011: "There's so much I love about London ... its grittiness, the cultural diversity." (Hear, hear). "I live in Shoreditch now and it's my favourite part of town. The City itself is fantastic too, particularly at weekends when it's empty. I love the juxtaposition of the old and the new."

Dave Wheeler who I know from Aon and from Ace Insurance grew up in Wapping and had a friend at school who lived inside the grounds of the Tower of London. As lock-up time was strictly 10pm – no messing, when the Crown Jewels are to be protected – the friend sometimes had to crash at Dave's house for the night! Meanwhile the legendary Sid Ellis would always offer that his family connection with the Tower of London was as useful as Heineken lager, for he could wangle you a visit where you'd be shown the Parts that Ordinary Tourists Don't Reach. (The legend about Sid was that he had once become so enraged with a broker that he had thrown the broker's file out through the office window).

The City of London has two famous ex-residents who are respectively buried and commemorated in Poets Corner at Westminster Abbey. They are separated by a span of six centuries. Born circa 1341, Geoffrey Chaucer was raised in Thames Street, the son of a wealthy merchant who ran a wine-importing business. He knew the City of London waterfront well: his poems included many of the phrases that he would have heard while the wines of Gascony were being unloaded at Three Cranes Wharf: "Come off, man ... lat see now ... namoore of this ... what say ye ... take hede now ... Jakke fool!" (I will leave you to imagine what that last one would be, in modern-day vernacular).

In 1347 Chaucer became a page at the court of King Edward III:

to use football terminology it was a "transfer" to Westminster, for we must remember that the walled-off City of London – the original Roman settlement of *Londinium* – was in those days a distinct and separate place from Westminster. But if you adjust the digits slightly, to make the year 1374, where was Chaucer then? Answer: back in the City to take the office of controller of the wool custom. It was one of the most prestigious posts in the Port of London: in effect he was quality-controlling the merchandise and ensuring its legitimacy.

Sir John Betjeman (1906 – 1984), poet and broadcaster, was a national treasure. He came to live in Cloth Fair, near the Barbican, in the 1960s after leaving the matrimonial home in the Cotswolds. He was appointed Poet Laureate in 1972. He saw out his last days living in Chelsea and Cornwall. I associate him very much with my working life in the City: for example, I have come to appreciate the City's rich and historic architecture but I wouldn't know the half of it without all of Betjeman's prose and poetry that has informed me.

Let's take railway and tube stations, for example. Writing in the 1950s of the two railway stations that have long been my alighting point from Orpington on commuting weekdays, it might be said that Betjeman's unflattering description of London Bridge station was as true then as it is now. What a creaking old rag-bag of a station it remained, during all my forty-six years of working in the City! It is only as recently as 2012 that commuters have seen the announcement of a long overdue large-scale plan to modernise the station. Notwithstanding the expected huge disruption of the railway timetable for several months –a disruption that I have rather luckily avoided by retiring from work in early 2013! – there will surely be a big sigh of relief to see the last of what Betjeman described more than sixty years ago as a shattered collection of girders and temporary-looking platforms. Meanwhile of Cannon Street station, Betjeman in the 1950s praised the pleasing visual effect of the two towers and cupolas at the river opening of the station. He declared that they blend well with the steepled outline of the City. Some twenty years ago the interior of the station was much modernised, to excellent and efficient effect, and I'd guess that Betjeman would be pleased to know that the exterior – in his opinion, a grand structure – was left largely intact.

In 2006 a locomotive running the Liverpool Street to Norfolk line was named after Betjeman, to thank him for persuading the developers to preserve part of the historic roof when the dark and dirt-encrusted old Liverpool Street station was thoroughly modernised in the 1980s. He had described the old terminus as "Civil engineer's Gothic ... with quite a resemblance to an ancient abbey." Betjeman was a fervent conservationist: a tireless and often successful campaigner to save precious old buildings from the axe. While he lived in the City of London he was a contributor to the regular column 'Nooks and Corners of the New Barbarism' in 'Private Eye' magazine that identified architectural or town planning outrages in various parts of Britain and railed against the folly or greed of the local councils and the developers.

Betjeman sounded a wistful note at the conclusion of his poem 'The Death of Aldersgate Station' when noting that the era of steam and gas-light was fading and would soon be lost. His poems of that ilk are a poignant reminder to me that I have seen great change in the City of London in my lifetime, just as Betjeman did in his. The generation gap dictates that Betjeman nostalgically recalls London railway stations of Victorian brick and iron and stone where tin-plate advertisements on the walls spoke of IRON JELLOIDS and IDRIS TABLE WATERS. The default position always for Betjeman, it seems, was to denounce all change and renovation as "desecration": for my part, as a commuter comparing the then-and-now on the railways since 1966 I'd have to welcome the modernisation of the lines, the stations and the carriages, especially the no-smoking rule (and Please! can there also be a no-mobile phones rule!). There have been days, of course, when I have cursed the rail service with words that aren't in The Bible – which commuter hasn't? – but to save on my suit-cleaning bills and also to gain some brownie points environmentally, the time came during my City working life when I ceased to hanker for Betjeman's fondly-remembered sooty tunnels and clouds of steam.

CITY OF LONDON FESTIVAL
6-18 JULY 1986

A MESSAGE FROM THE LORD MAYOR ...

"Today's City skyline may be dominated by the soaring office towers of the commercial world, but at ground level the City remains as proud as ever of its musical theatrical and artistic traditions.

"The annual City of London Festival provides a most welcome opportunity for City workers and their guests to celebrate their love of Arts in venues as varied and wonderful as the works to be performed and enjoyed."

Sir Allan Davis, The Right Hon The Lord Mayor of London, President of the City Arts Trust.

DANIEL DEFOE

On the evening of 19 May 2010 I spent a most enjoyable and interesting evening in the company of Mr Daniel Defoe.

As it was Daniel Defoe's 350th birthday that day, I must ask you to understand that he was unable to be there in person! But, thanks to the enthusiasm of four volunteer readers from the City of London Libraries staff (two male, two female) the audience was treated to a lively selection of readings of Defoe's works, interspersed with biographical facts about his life.

My favourite Gwendoline Butler detective thriller story is 'The Interlopers' (Geoffrey Bles, 1959). Defoe's book 'Journal of the Plague Year' (1665) features in the plot. However, as 'The Interloper' is long out of print, and the late Ms Butler (died 2013) has faded in prominence as a crime fiction author, I had no expectation that she or her book would warrant any mention from the four presenters at the lecture. I was absolutely right – there was no mention.

Be kind to foreigners, debtors, women…

The lecture was styled as 'An evening's celebration to mark the 350th year of the birth of Daniel Defoe'. The poster for the lecture headlined Defoe as "A True-born Englishman". That was certainly true. He was born on the north side of the City of London, in 1660. However, it was in irony that he coined the phrase "A True-Born Englishman". He used it as the title of one of his best-known political pamphlets. An extract from it was one of the first readings that we heard from the presenters. Defoe argued (in 1697) that before an Englishman gets too high and mighty, and looks down upon foreigners as unworthies and undesirables, he should pause to remember where his "Englishness" actually comes from. Why, from a mix of Celts, Danes, Normans, Picts, Romans, Scots and Saxons: invaders, savages and plunderers all!

We heard an extract too from Defoe's plea for leniency to debtors. Hmm – if he were to air that sentiment today, in the aftermath of the "credit crunch", I wonder what sort of reception he would get?

The very first reading was taken from Defoe's essay 'On the Education of Women'. In this, Defoe claimed that it was barbarous for a civilised and Christian country to deny the advantages of learning to women. He found it surprising that they managed to be conversible at all, bearing in mind that their youth had customarily to be spent learning how to stitch and sew, or make baubles. He expressed confidence that if women were allowed to have the same standard of education as men, they should no longer deserve reproach for their folly and impertinence: indeed, he declared that "they might be guilty of less than us."

I chuckled silently while listening to this, for it so happened that a few days before attending the lecture I had been re-reading some old copies of 'Chess' magazine. I had been reminded that the readers letters page had conducted over several months an interesting debate of the possible reasons why men evidently play chess much better than women.

It had been my former school friend (and fellow member of the school chess club) Malcolm Burn who had neatly wrapped up the discussion. Writing from his London W9 address in June 1973, Malcolm had firstly demonstrated his bookish erudition by citing two fictional chess-playing incidents that the female authors George Eliot and Virginia Woolf had included in their respective novels 'Felix Holt' and 'The Voyage Out'. Malcolm had then stated:

"… The female imagination does not readily confine itself within a rigid and artificial framework of rules which exclude the interplay of human emotions and social relationships. …It is no criticism of women to say that they are less successful than men at chess; it may even be a compliment to their emotional stability and maturity."

I think that Defoe would have approved.

Pamphleteer and novelist

Defoe was evidently a writer who liked to throw in everything including the kitchen sink; as though by sheer weight of words he could wear down the reader, and incline the reader to his own point of view. The lead presenter informed us that Defoe's collected published works ran to fourteen volumes. In his early days of political and religious zeal, he was a Whig and a Protestant. One especially inflammatory religious tract earned him a sentence to stand in the pillory, in 1703. Unabashed, he wrote and published a long – very, very long – poem 'Hymn to the Pillory'. According to some accounts, many copies were sold, and the public turned out to laud Defoe as a hero and throw symbolic flowers at him, instead of pelting him with rotten fruit and rubbish. However, it didn't save him from a spell inside Newgate Prison, afterwards.

It was not until much later that Defoe took up story-writing. His famous 'Robinson Crusoe' was published in 1719 when he was 59 years old. Some literary historians regard Defoe as a founder of the English novel. I know that as a child I knew well the story of the shipwrecked Robinson Crusoe and his faithful servant, Man Friday. However, I cannot pinpoint how I knew it. Did my parents read it to me, or give me a children's abridged version of the book to read? Everyone at school knew the story. I wonder whether it is still today a standard classic that all children know? - or has it been sacrificed on the modern-day altar of "political correctness"?

'A Journal of the Plague Year'

Aldgate, not far from the present-day Lloyd's building, was one of the worst City of London districts to be hit by the Great Plague. Dead bodies piled up everywhere. Defoe published his famous book in 1722. Today, we would call it "faction" – a fictionalised account of a real event. Defoe was only five years old when the Great Plague struck London in 1665, so he couldn't have written a first-hand account of living through it, as did Samuel Pepys of course.

The author Gwendoline Butler was an Oxford-educated history scholar. For me, one of the essential qualities of her detective story books is the skilful and informative weaving of English social history (especially London social history) into her stories and plots. Nowhere does she master this better than in 'The Interlopers'. Abbie, a young American student, rents a flat in the Borough district of London, next to the Thames, while researching the history of the English baronetcy in the sixteenth and seventeenth centuries. One of the books that she finds on the shelf inside the flat is Defoe's 'Journal of the Plague Year'. After reading it, Abbie's mind is flooded by the notion that "London was peopled with ghosts: the ghosts of people who had listened with terror to the bell tolling for them, who had seen the funeral carts roll away, and looked into the pits of the dead."

Abbie draws a deep breath and muses that in Borough itself the plague would not have been so deadly, for it was south of the river, where (as I once wrote in a poem of mine):

> … The Thames was met
> As meadows sloped to Horsleydown.

At this point in the story, the reader learns from the knowledgeable Ms Butler that Abbie does not realise that unfortunately the plague was carried by boats and therefore the pedlars and travellers that had passed through what they had hoped was the safety of the green fields of Southwark had not in fact escaped.

If I had been too busy to attend the Defoe lecture, and I had wanted the 'Just a Minute' version of his life story, I could have read in 'The Interlopers' that Defoe, the first great journalist, the begetter of the novel, the student of 'Roxana' and 'Moll Flanders', had stood in the pillory and had died poor.

Yes, in common with many famous artists, composers and writers, Defoe battled with poverty in real life. A fair biographer should not try to hide the flaws in Defoe's character, nor should it be omitted that some of his actions marked him out as a scoundrel and a swindler. But in the ultimate reckoning, the "True-born Englishmen" was a hero – for he made English literature rich with his legacy.

WORDSWORTH'S TREE IN WOOD STREET, CHEAPSIDE

William Wordsworth placed his poem 'The Reverie of Poor Susan' in a City of London setting – specifically in Cheapside, where he lodged briefly in 1791, quite close to St Paul's Cathedral. He was aged twenty-one.

Wordsworth spent very little time in London, during his life. He was a native of Cumberland. He lived mostly in the Lake District, and died there at the age of eighty. As a young man, after completing his education at Cambridge, he became restless, and he didn't settle into a job. He roamed around the UK and Europe. During his stopovers in London, he was politically active. He attended debates in Parliament, and he liked to voice his own opinions at public debates and lectures.

'The Reverie of Poor Susan' was published in the second edition of 'Lyrical Ballads' dated 1800. The book was a joint effort by Wordsworth and Samuel Taylor Coleridge, who had become friends. They vowed to forsake long-winded poetry that was full of classical references and allegory. They sought to write poems that used simple and direct conversational language.

The book was sensationally successful, and the poems established the reputations of these two now universally famous poets.

>At the corner of Wood Street, when daylight appears,
>Hangs a thrush that sings loud, it has sung for
>three years:
>Poor Susan has passed by the spot, and has heard
>In the silence of morning the song of the bird.
>
>'Tis a note of enchantment; what ails her? She sees
>A mountain ascending, a vision of trees;
>Bright volumes of vapour through Lothbury glide,

And a river flows on through the vale of Cheapside.

Green pastures she views in the midst of the dale,
Down which she so often has tripped with her pail;
And a single small cottage, a nest like a dove's,
The only one dwelling on earth that she loves.

She looks, and her heart is in heaven: but they fade,
The mist and the river, the hill and the shade:
The stream will not flow, and the hill will not rise,
And the colours have all passed away from her eyes.

I wonder if your reaction, on first reading this poem, will be the same as mine when I first read it? I was startled by the crass simplicity of the poem. It seemed barely to rise above doggerel; and surely some of the rhymes were excruciating? – verse three, in particular?

My reaction was much to my discredit. It highlighted my ignorance of the significant role that Wordsworth and Coleridge occupy in the history and development of British poetry.

We must hail the poem for its important historical context. Critics have suggested that the dramatic effect of the 'Lyrical Ballads' upon English literature in the late eighteenth-century can be likened to rock n'roll first arriving in Britain during the 1950s, or the birth of punk rock in the late 1970s!"

Today in Wood Street, off Cheapside, Wordsworth's poem 'Poor Susan' is commemorated by an informative inscription on an outdoor wooden board. There is an information reference too in the Centre for Metropolitan History, mentioning that the tree was for a long time the residence of rooks. It is surmised that one summer morning while Wordsworth was walking along Cheapside he had seen the plane-tree at the corner of Wood Street wave its branches to him, and this had triggered a poetic imagination of some poor Cumberland servant-girl toiling in London, and pining for her faraway home among the pleasant hills.

What truly was in Wordsworth's mind when he composed the 'Poor Susan' poem we can indeed only guess: on the other hand, if we want to know what he and his family were doing on the 17 June 1798 there is no need for guesswork, for we know it exactly from a letter that Dorothy Wordsworth wrote to Mrs Rawson (her former nanny). They were planning to move house! She wrote that they had determined to go to Germany, along with Mr and Mrs Coleridge and their family. She expressed the intention to travel as far within Europe as "the tether of our scanty income shall permit". To assist them in this ambition she hoped to supplement their financial resources by carrying out English and German translation work, if any could be found. She added the slightly negative comment that "translation is the most profitable species of literary labour." Negative – yes; but hers was a realistic comment, as many a struggling author would know from bitter experience! Fortunately for the Wordsworths fame and fortune was soon to come to them, even if they were penny-pinched in mid-1798.

As regards 'Poor Susan' and the tree, I will pause to state that Wordsworth placed an imaginary thrush there, and not a rook, but much more importantly, let us celebrate the minor miracle that in built-up Cheapside, the tree is still there today.

It can be taken as read, I'm sure, that in the 1790s the view from the corner of Wood Street and Cheapside, looking north to St Paul's Cathedral in the near foreground, was magnificent in its beauty. The view of the cathedral is mercifully not blocked today by any intervening building or other obstruction, but, the poor old tree in Wood Street has not exactly been mollycoddled. It survives; but only just, one feels. It stands in a rather drab railed-off yard, hemmed in on three sides by high-walled buildings that starve its lower trunk of natural light. Its upper branches fortunately do escape over the top of the brickwork, to fill the Cheapside skyline with richly-coloured leaf.

The City of London: Wandering and Wondering

Wordsworth's tree in Wood Street, off Cheapside.

BLUE PLAQUES AND STATUES

What was your reaction when you heard the news in January 2013 that blue plaques had become another of the many victims of the so-called "austerity" cost-cutting in Britain? English Heritage declared that it would have to stop its blue plaque scheme, commemorating the former residences of famous people, because government funding cuts had made it impossible to continue.

Did you think, as I immediately did: "Oh well, in that case I won't bother now to become a famous doctor / musician / politician / scientist / writer! What would be the point, if I'm not going to be commemorated with a blue plaque!"

Rest easy: better news has quickly followed. Blue plaques may have suffered a significant stumble but they don't appear to be out for the count. English Heritage has announced that pre-existing promises, at least, will be met. And that has already meant that a plaque has been duly erected to Harry Beck, who designed (in 1930) the iconic London underground tube map. That is indeed an appropriate action in 2013, to coincide with the 150th anniversary of the opening of London's first tube line.

If you live in the City of London and you rather fancy having a blue plaque erected outside your home, even if it probably will be a posthumous honour, which horse should you back? By this I mean: which professional or artistic path should you take in life, for best chance of your name becoming sufficiently elite to be commemorated?

After studying the list of blue plaques that are sited in the City of London it is my recommendation that unless you are a writer your best bet is to take the cloth and be a Reverend!

Writers and Churchmen

Let's take the writers first. Two famous Samuels haunt opposite ends of the City. If you take the well-trodden tourist path along the narrow alley beside the famous Cheshire Cheese pub in Fleet Street - and I have, myself, supped some ale inside that pub when accompanying American visitors to that tourist shrine! - you will find that one of the elegant buildings in the streets and courtyards concealed behind the Cheshire Cheese is the Samuel Johnson House. Many biographers have written of Samuel Johnson. He towers over the history of the English language: during an eight-year period of the mid-1800s he put together the English Dictionary and for that feat alone he goes up on a pedestal for a self-confessed word-worshipper like me! My favourite book about Johnson is Beryl Bainbridge's fictional (factional) 'According to Queeney' (Abacus, 2002): it is a decidedly "warts-and-all" portrait of the great man of letters but it is a brilliant evocation of period London.

Meanwhile at the eastern end of the City, amongst the Admiralty office buildings near the Tower of London (in which he was once briefly imprisoned) the famous diarist Samuel Pepys recorded his life and work, his travels and his marital ups-and-downs. Thanks to his easy, chatty style of writing, his diary has lived on and gives us a far better idea of what life was really like in the reign of Charles II than any formal history book could do. Pepys (1633 - 1703) is buried at St Olave's in Hart Street. During my time of working in the City it was an occasional pleasure to take a sandwich lunch into the quiet little park in Seething Lane situated near to the house where Pepys once lived, close by to the Navy office where he worked as a senior official.

In the City you can find blue plaques for the poets John Betjeman, John Keats and Alexander Pope. Betjeman lived near Smithfield Market in a small street with the delightful name of Cloth Fair. I'd even go so far as to say of the name Cloth Fair that "A thing of beauty is a joy for ever." That, of course, is a famous line by the great Romantic poet Keats! - he studied in London at the joint school of Guy's and St Thomas's Hospital, but his intended career as a surgeon was soon overtaken by his literary fame. Just outside the City if you walk past the Law Courts and head along the south side of Strand then just before you reach Waterloo Bridge you'll find a most interesting window display of several luminaries from all walks of life who once passed through the portals of medical school: in addition to Keats they include the politician David Owen whose former house in Limehouse became an everyday sight for me as a motorist when proceeding at snail's pace along Narrow Street during the brief period in the early 1990s when I worked in Docklands.

Alexander Pope wrote 'The Rape of the Lock' in 1712: he is dubbed as Poet of "The Age of Reason" but I'd politely have to say that his work is rather hard-going for modern-day readers. I must reluctantly say the same of Charles Lamb and his 'Essays of Elia' (1823). Some years ago I gleefully purchased a lovely leather-bound vintage edition of this book: eventually my verdict was that it has a nice swanky presence on my bookshelf at home, but umm - try reading it! Lamb's blue plaque is found in Temple (this legal quarter of the City contains some of its most serene and scenic alleyways and open spaces) and Pope's is in Lombard Street.

The identification of deserving candidates for blue plaque memorials in the City of London has included some serious harking back to long ago. This process has thrown up recondite poets such as Robert Bloomfield. He was something of a "one-hit wonder" when his rustic poem 'The Farmer's Boy' became all the rage in 1800. His blue plaque is displayed in Telegraph Street.

I don't know if William Curtis qualifies as a writer, exactly: he wrote books about botany and he is duly commemorated in Gracechurch Street. Edward Edwards has his plaque in Idol Lane. He was not a writer but he certainly was a man of books, for in the Victorian era he championed the introduction of public libraries. So up he goes on a pedestal for me, in gratitude for that far from idle achievement in his lifetime!

Religion plays a good few aces in the City when it comes to blue plaques. John Wesley founded the Methodist Church: his chapel stands in City Road and his blue plaque is there, too. His younger brother Charles Wesley has a blue plaque in nearby Little Britain.

The birthplaces of St Thomas A'Becket and Cardinal John Henry Newman are respectively marked in Cheapside and Threadneedle Street, while the Reverend Clayton (founder of Toc H) is memorialised in Trinity Square. By fond repute "Tubby" Clayton was the archetypal absent-minded and bumbling cleric – so might we imagine that the actor Derek Nimmo of 'Gas and Gaiters' fame could have suitably portrayed him? – or might we instead see Michael Hordern as best man for the role, perhaps?

On the basis that being either a writer or churchman is a good ticket for ending up with your name on a blue plaque in the City, the precocious young Thomas Chatterton ticked both boxes! - but his is a tragic story, for in 1770 he committed suicide (by arsenic) at the age of only seventeen. His religious poems had nevertheless already made his reputation - a sufficient one for him later to earn a blue plaque near Holborn where he had resided in the City of London. Too shy to write under his own name at first, he had adopted while living in Bristol the pseudonym of a fifteenth-century monk. Chatterton is another person brought engagingly to life by the author Peter Ackroyd whose book 'Chatterton' (currently available in paperback from Abacus) was first published in 1987.

Statues and Sundries

Statues and busts of all shapes and sizes can be found in the City of London. It's my impression that once we have eliminated the royal statues and the numerous types of war memorials we are left with a sumptuous selection of sundries to find and enjoy.

Some statues are mounted high up on grand buildings and structures or are snuggled into wall recesses. Sir Thomas Gresham is a leading example: one statue of him stands in the south-facing structure of Holborn Viaduct and another is cut into an exterior wall of the Royal Exchange. Sir Thomas is widely commemorated in the City: there is his blue plaque in Old Broad Street, while Gresham Street and Gresham College bear his name. Moreover, when you see the shiny gold grasshopper crest above a coat of arms in Lombard Street, it is his.

An acquaintance of the royal Elizabethan court, Sir Thomas Gresham was a rich merchant. He belonged to the Mercers Company: the highest esteemed of all the Livery Companies in the City. His most visible legacy to the City is surely the Royal Exchange building at the top of Cornhill and Threadneedle Street. He founded it in 1565, modelled upon the Bourse in Antwerp. It would have its ups and downs – literally! – for it burnt down in 1666 and again in 1838 (while serving as headquarters of Lloyd's of London insurance). Pepys had diarised Charles II laying the foundation stone of the second building. So the present-day bricks and mortar Royal Exchange with the imposing Palladian frontage is version three of Sir Thomas Gresham's grand concept to build a commercial trading centre in the heart of the City.

When I first came to the City to work in 1966 war damage had left the grand old edifice in need of the glitzy interior facelift and revitalisation that it now revels in: all the top international brand names in gift-shops and fine-dining can be found at the Royal Exchange now. Amidst all this opulent high-spending on jewellery, luggage and other luxury commodities it might seem rather incongruous that the statue of George Peabody, famous American philanthropist and benefactor to the poor, is sited just beside the Royal Exchange! But Peabody was a man of commerce too: he made his fortune as a manufacturer before moving to London in 1837 to become a financier.

Let me now pose a question: if statues of Britannia, St George and the Dragon, and Old Father Thames are to be sited in our country, what is the most fitting place for them? I'd say that the City of London is the exact right and proper place. The authorities have evidently thought along the same lines as me on this, and so if you venture into the respective districts of Old Billingsgate Hall, Blackfriars and Trinity Square, you'll find these particular statues.

At the opposite end of the spectrum, away from such grand patriotic symbols of old legend, the City pays tribute to two of its intrinsic professions by way of generic statutes sited very close to each other in Cannon Street. I'm a bit dubious about these two statues, though. The more recent of them, unveiled in 2011, stands inside Cannon Street railway station and might be thought to rather inconveniently get in the way of passengers swarming away from or towards Platforms 5 to 8? But it's hard to dislike the earnest young face of The Plumber's Apprentice as we become reminded that plumbing – in its full pomp The Worshipful Company of Plumbers - is not only a modern profession but is one of the City's most ancient traditional skills.

The other statue that I'm referring to is representative of the relatively new profession of futures trading: new in the sense of being a Johnny Come Lately form of financial trading, but age-old in the broader sense that financial activity has taken place in many shapes and forms in the City throughout many centuries of time. The lifelike statue of The LIFFE Trader has recently been removed to the Guildhall but when first unveiled in 1997 it stood on the pavement in Walbrook opposite Cannon Street railway station. The statue depicts a young male trader speaking into his mobile phone. Ah – but what might he be saying? In light of recent allegations of rate-fixing and other shady goings-on in the banking world, is it tempting for us to be cynical when we invent a possible conversation that might be taking place on his phone?

Again with statues we can note that writing and religion is well represented in the City: in addition to names that I have already mentioned such as Thomas A'Becket, Charles and John Wesley there are the Black Friar in, er, Blackfriars; the two friars in, er, Crutched Friars; the poet John Donne at St Paul's Cathedral, John Milton at the Victoria Embankment and in St Giles Cripplegate: oh, and someone called William Shakespeare, no less, in Aldermanbury.

Aside from scribes and sky pilots, a small shout at getting yourself a blue plaque in the City is to have a surname ending with the letter 'i'? It worked for Benjamin Disraeli the Prime Minister, for Joseph Grimaldi the clown, for Gugliemo Marconi the inventor and for Guiseppe Mazzini the Italian patriot. With a name like Guiseppe Mazzini if he were not a real-life person he might have been one of the fictional characters invented by one of the leading authors of adventure thriller stories in the early twentieth-century? The famous author that I am referring to is Edgar Wallace (1875 – 1932) whose crime stories exploited the mystique of faraway foreign countries. Although we might today find his outrageous stereotyping of national characteristics to be jarring, in his own lifetime it was his successful trademark to colour his fiction stories with exotic international heroes and villains such as the inscrutable Mr Feng Ho. He placed his characters in romantic overseas settings that must have made compelling reading for his large number of readers who had never, in those days, seen anything of Africa, the Far East and such far-off lands, save for artists' illustrations in books.

Wallace was an international news reporter and war correspondent by profession. When the Daily Mail journalist Tom Utley won an industry prize in May 2011, awarded to him at the London Press Club, his prize was named the Edgar Wallace Award. I consider it to be splendid that the name of Wallace is perpetuated in this way. Wallace is commemorated in a bronze wall-plaque in Fleet Street, and Paul Julius Reuter, another great doyen of the news industry, warrants a granite statue there too.

Some of the famous people that are commemorated in the City have no special category beyond eminence in their own individual field. Do we instinctively think that the Swiss led the world in the making of watches and clocks? ("We have ways of making you tock.") Maybe they did: but in the City – again in Fleet Street - we see a blue plaque for Thomas Tompion (1639 – 1713) "The Father of English Clockmaking". As a word-lover, I instinctively wish and hope that he invented something that was branded 'The Thomas Tompion Timepiece'! – but I find no evidence, alas, that this ever happened!

At the beginning of this article I mentioned that Harry Beck has received a blue plaque to honour his name in connection with the London Underground. One of the City of London's more unexpected and indeed large statues, I warrant, is to be found in Cornhill and enjoys a special significance in the year 2013 that marks the 150th anniversary of the London Underground. Facing towards St Paul's Cathedral, route map in his hand, the great Victorian "burrower" James Henry Greathead announces himself on his plinth that he was Chief Engineer and "Inventor of the Travelling Shield that made possible the cutting of the tunnels for London's deep level tube system." The insignia of the Southern Railway lends credence to his important role. Born in South Africa, he settled and worked in London. He led numerous railway projects in and around the capital city, and he acted as consultant for the building of the Blackwall Tunnel, too.

Am I the only person, I wonder, to sense a slight irony that the statue to JH Greathead is sited so that he is looking, in near foreground, at one of the most notorious road traffic bottlenecks in the City? For he stands in the very middle of the road, next to the Royal Exchange at the end of Cornhill, where the big roundabout above Bank tube station has six feeder roads: each one a main artery taking heavy traffic into and out of the very heart of the City of London's financial centre. Many are the frustrated motorists who might have read the inscription on JH Greathead's statue while stuck in the traffic.

Bearing in mind all the hustle and bustle that goes on in the City of London let me conclude by hailing one of its most deserving but unsung heroes. Blink as you're walking along Queen Victoria Street and you may miss Cleary Gardens, but tucked away inside its modest little collection of shrubs and flowers and greenery you'll find a blue plaque in honour of Fred Cleary (1905 – 1984) The inscription says: "Tireless in his wish to increase open space in the City." And so if you can dwell for a short while to sit there – Cleary Gardens is sited to give a pleasant view of the white Portland stone tower and lead spire of St Nicholas, Cole Abbey – it will be a fitting moment perhaps for appreciating why William Dunbar (born circa 1465) once declared: "London, thou art the flower of cities all!"

James Henry Greathead

The City of London: Wandering and Wondering

FINANCE

Tower 42 viewed from St Mary Axe with illuminated "Walking Men" in the foreground.

MANLEY HOPKINS, SON & COOKES - MARINE AVERAGE ADJUSTERS AND POETS

Sun Court, Cornhill, London EC3: A surprising literary connection.

If you walk the length of Cornhill in the heart of the City of London, you will be following some extremely famous literary footprints.

You might need to be eagle-eyed to spot the wall plaques marking the births of the celebrated poets Thomas Hood (1799 – 1845) and Thomas Gray (1716 – 1771).

Hood's blue plaque is sited at knee-height on a wall in Poultry, just before Cornhill becomes one of the roads that you can enter from the big roundabout at Bank. Hood is best known for his poem that begins: "I remember, I remember, the house where I was born." Well, should he return there today he'd find that the laburnum tree planted by his brother is no longer "living yet"! – but he might be consoled by the modern-day view of the grand stonework and frontages of the Bank of England, the Mansion House and the Royal Exchange.

Gray's birth-plaque rather perversely has black lettering on a black background, but if you stop and peer at it carefully you can discern the opening line of his immortal 'Elegy Written in a Country Churchyard'. Two fine churches stand close by in Cornhill, but embedded as they are amongst high-rise buildings, banks and shops, neither St Michael nor St Peter evoke a sense of Gray's country churchyard with its ploughman and its herd of cattle. Moreover, the noise of Cornhill's traffic would drown out the "beetle's droning flight and the swallow twittering from the straw-built shed"!

If you duck down one of the alleyways leading off Cornhill at its mid-length near to the two churches, you'll quickly find yourself in

Charles Dickens territory. In fact, the Victorian atmosphere and setting in those narrow byways is so perfectly preserved nowadays that you likely wouldn't bat an eyelid if you suddenly encountered Mr Pickwick strolling along and belching happily after downing his pint of porter at The George & Vulture chop house!

Several prominent literary figures worked in the vicinity of Cornhill, in various professions such as banking, insurance or the law. Charles Lamb, for example, walked to work from his home in Holborn every rush-hour morning, and back again at night, during the early 1800s. His workplace at the East India House stood just along from Cornhill in Leadenhall Street, close to the present-day Lloyd's insurance building. Charles Lamb didn't stop for a Starbs coffee or a designer-sandwich at Pret-a-Manger, but in Peter Ackroyd's fictional account of his life he did purchase a veal pie from a street-seller, to take into the office for his lunch

Let me mention to you now the little-known and perhaps rather surprising literary association that goes with one of the most colourful sights that you will see in Cornhill. Almost directly opposite the church of St Peter (Wren, late 1600s) you'll see a strikingly bright yellow circular sign, bearing the words 'Sun Court' in prominent black lettering. If you should happen to possess a copy of a most charming little book 'One Hundred Years of the Association of Average Adjusters 1869 to 1969' (published by W & J Mackay & Co, Chatham, in 1969), you will learn that Manley Hopkins, one of the lions of the profession of marine insurance, set up his office in the very same location that is Sun Court, today.

It was a new brass plate on the door of no. 69 Cornhill on 1st July 1844 that heralded the birth of a new company by the name of Manley, Hopkins, Son & Cookes. At the age of twenty-six the ambitious young Manley Hopkins had set up on his own as an average adjuster. In time, his technical knowledge and very considerable literary skill enabled him to write some leading textbooks. In his private time he was also a poet of some merit. His talents were inherited by three, at least, of his sons. Arthur and Everard achieved success with their illustrations to 'Punch' magazine, and the name of Gerard Manley Hopkins was to become famous, though not till thirty years after his death when his collected poems were first published in 1918.

From this you will gather that Manley Hopkins was not your average average adjuster. (I am truly sorry about the pun! – but I had to do it, didn't I?). He was not only a leading businessman, but a published author and poet too.

Manley Hopkins was not to know it during his own lifetime, but in terms of literary fame and achievement he was to be completely overshadowed by his son Gerard Manley Hopkins. Born in 1844, at Stratford in East London, Gerard Manley Hopkins was the first of the nine children of Manley and his wife Catherine. Manley senior had published a volume of poetry in 1843. Much later the firstborn son was to become one of the world's most celebrated and popular poets.

Marine insurance and poetry ... two unlikely bedfellows, some might say? Sadly, it doesn't seem that any of the published poetry of Manley Hopkins senior is still around today. Well, I haven't been able to find any. However, I wonder if you might be willing to indulge me in a little premise of mine, that the rich language of a marine insurance policy is a poetry in itself?

Here is an example of the "poetry" that a marine adjusting clerk would dutifully have written at his desk in the early 1800s. He would have written it in a flowing copperplate hand, and his firm would have employed copywriters - always male - whose laborious but devoted task it was to write duplicate, virtually photographic copies of his original. Some of the adjustment statements were lithographed on to stone, and surviving copies today can be regarded almost as beautiful works of art!

"STATEMENT OF GENERAL AND PARTICULAR AVERAGE, per Gregory, J. Lune, from Liverpool to the Mediterranean:

... Occasioned by springing a leak at sea, and, in consequence, cutting away a part of her main stern-post and transom-beam, by which means, it is said, she stopped the leak, and was thereby enabled to return to Liverpool ... James Page & Co Shipwrights bill £1,168 14s 11d ..."

From comparatively humble beginnings, the marine average adjusting profession gradually improved its standing in society. The evidence for this is the choice of hotels at which the Association held its annual dinner. In the 1870s and 1880s the venues included the likes of The London Tavern and The Albion, Aldersgate Street. Come the 1900s and grander hotels in the West End started to be used, culminating in the use from 1935 onwards of the Mayfair, Claridges or the Savoy.

One of the star exhibits in Mr Wilson's book is a copy of the menu for the annual dinner of 1884. Manley Hopkins and his Victorian colleagues must have had hearty appetites and a good deal of stamina to get through all of the following! -

- Thick Spring Soup
- Dorees a l'Italienne
- Salmon
- Whitebait
- Escallopes de Ris de Veau aux Petit Pois
- Poulet a l'Eclarte
- Chines of Mutton
- Ham and Salad
- Ducklings, Goslings, Asparagus
- Fruit Jellies, Pastry
- Ratafia Creams, Compotes of Oranges
- Ice Pudding

Whew!

Life – and the world – has moved on a long way since then. If you walk along Cornhill today it is perfectly possible that on a high floor of a nearby office building, a marine insurance adjuster is sending an e-mail from his or her workstation. Via satellite the information flashes to the other side of the world and the recipient is instantly informed of the estimated amount of damage to the supertanker that yesterday developed engine trouble in the Indian Ocean and had to put into port unexpectedly.

That said, the Lloyd's and London insurance market of today is split into three business sectors – aviation, marine and non-marine. Of these three, it is always the marine market that has somehow never quite lost its label of being an old-fashioned and slow-paced institution. One suspects that instead of issuing policies electronically, they'd rather be scratching them out on parchment with a quill pen, then affixing a wax seal and a sevenpenny stamp while perusing that day's 'Lloyd's List' newspaper (founded 1734) to check all the shipping movements. And whenever someone in the marine department needs to know the time, rather than press a button on their hand-held Blackberry, they would prefer to consult their gold watch on a chain, produced with a flourish from their waistcoat pocket.

I am not confident that I can persuade you to see a marine insurance policy as "poetry". I can hear your depth-chargers exploding into my side, to sink my theory. Defiantly, though, with my last breath before I drown, I will protest to you that any document containing such delights as the Blocking and Trapping Clause, the Sue and Labour clause (nothing to do with maternity), the Bottom Treatment Clause (nothing to do with film stars, or WAGs) or the Violent Theft, Piracy and Barratry Exclusion, is surely the purest poetry?

I will develop this theory further. When you were at school did the teacher sometimes start a lesson by reading out the first few lines of a story? – and afterwards instruct each pupil to make up and write a follow-on?

If so, imagine getting this as the opening of your story: "Beginning the adventure upon the vessel, and so shall continue and endure during the period, as employment may offer, in port or at sea, in docks and graving docks, and on ways, gridirons and pontoons ..."

I am inclined to think that I would go on from there and write something like: "Yo! Ho! Ho! and a bottle of rum!" But what you have just read above is not the opening paragraph of a Robert Louis Stevenson swashbuckling sea-tale, nor a Midshipman Hornblower. Believe it or not, it is the first part of the Adventure Clause that is commonly found in marine insurance policies. I am not making this up: it truly is. And I don't mean marine insurance policies from long ago: I have copied the above very words from a Lloyd's policy dated 2011.

If the marine insurance market in London characterises the construction of an insurance policy as Beginning an Adventure, they surely must have a touch of poetry in their soul? Now it is on the record that Francis (F.R.) Bussell, a venerable underwriter at Lloyd's one hundred years ago, told his lawyers always to use simple and clear language when drafting the policies. "Away with your 'whereases' and your 'hereinbeforesaids', etc." But I'm all for a bit of rich and flowery language every now and then, myself. Let's have some "Perils of the Seas, Men-of-War, Fire, Lightning, Earthquake, Enemies, Pirates, Rovers, Assailing Thieves, Jettisons, Letters of Mart and Counter-Mart, Surprisals, Takings at Sea, Arrests, Restraints and Detainments of all Kings, Princes and Peoples," to brighten up the insurance market! (I'm still reading from that policy dated 2011, by the way).

I am no champion of obfuscation. I know that it is sometimes necessary for insurance policy wordings to be complex. But fie on obscurity: it is exquisite wordery that I crave! The legal profession can give the marine insurance market a run for its money when it comes to flamboyant word-crafting: I don't mean all their Latin stuff like *res ipsa loquitur* because that's cheating: one of my favourite things to read is a writ that has been served in the American courts where the plaintiff "prays for relief "– usually in the multi-million dollars, which is the sort of relief that is <u>worth</u> praying for – but then in reply "Comes Now John Doe, defendant…" And for the beauty of that "Comes Now" I reckon that he automatically should win the case, on fine-wordery alone.

Let me conclude at the opposite extreme. You must know the expression A1 meaning first rate: the very best. It is the ultimate in alpha-numerical brevity. And guess where it comes from? – Lloyd's insurance! It originates from the Shipping Register, to classify a first class ship and a first class risk.

POETRY IN THE CITY

My friend John Preston at *www.prestonspoetry.co.uk*

Shame on you Alan Bennett, famous author and playwright, for mocking the insurance profession and doubting that any creative writers can be numbered in our ranks. OK, I know it was only gentle mockery, but even if Mr Bennett didn't know of Manley Hopkins, marine adjuster and poet, he surely must have known of the famous American poet Wallace Stevens who was the vice president of an insurance company. (I have visited the headquarters of his company, the Hartford Insurance in Connecticut, One of the present-day commemorations of Stevens in Hartford is the Wallace Stevens Walk. The route retraces his two-mile daily commute to and from his workplace in the 1930s. At strategic points during the re-enactment walk, everyone stops and a verse is recited aloud from one of his best-known poems 'Thirteen Ways of Looking at a Blackbird'.)

Foremost verse-spinner today in the London insurance and reinsurance market is my friend John Preston. John used to work for the Policy Signing & Accounting Centre (PSAC) which itself should surely be the opening line of a limerick, although I'm not volunteering myself to write it! John now works for a Lloyd's underwriting syndicate.

I caught on to John's flair for composing poetry several years ago when he asked me to tell him my wife's first name or my children's first names. He explained that he often would knock up a little poem or ditty for his family, his friends, his children's friends, etc, incorporating a personal touch of including the person's name in the poem. Later he was to show me the truth of this when he kindly gave me five neatly-produced and self-published books (1993) in which there were many examples of his said poems. The one that always sticks in my mind, and I don't have to search my bookshelves indoors to be reminded of it, is his poem that begins:

Nicholas thought it ridiculous ...

I have recently found and re-read these books and I am reminded of other titles and excellent poems such as 'Mr Grumpy Groany'. As you may easily guess, these books and poems of John's are aimed very much at young children – and my wife will testify that when she has read aloud from John's books in her classroom, the pupils have been readily engaged.

John's subsequent published works include a poetic tribute to the stately home of Audley End, a Verse History of Britain, and two business books about project and lifestyle management: one in prose and the other ('The Verse Advice I Can Give You') in rhyme. John dispenses it all with a twinkle in his eye, and he donates all his sales receipts to Great Ormond Street Hospital. Look on his website for details. And if you need a public orator, especially with some poetry to be spouted, send for John! He can readily spin some humorous verse about topical subjects in the Lloyd's insurance market. If you twist his arm you might even get him to do his 'Satchmo' impression: a melodious tune on his trumpet, Louis Armstrong style.

John Preston

'Poetry in the City' is an organisation that seeks out poetry-writers from the rank and file of office workers. Committee member Frances Hughes, a lawyer, has stated: "If you have a very stressful life, reading poetry is a manageable art form to fit around a job." Another member Mr Cavendish-Jones, also a lawyer, has pointed out that contrary to public opinion lawyers don't deliberately try to express things obscurely: "A good lawyer is someone who can make something very clear without any excess verbiage … composing poetry as a hobby can help with this."

If we accept the notion that "poets and lawyers share a precise use of language", where does that leave the likes of John Preston and myself, as flag-bearers for the insurance profession? I remember one evening when I was in a friend's house during my sixth form schooldays. For some reason that I can't imagine, the subject of insurance came up when we were talking to her Dad. He expressed the thought that one of the most interesting and skilled jobs in insurance must surely be the drafting of a policy wording. He evidently pictured this as being a role that insurance companies would seek to fill with nothing less than a William Shakespeare, so deft would be the standard of craftsmanship required.

If I recall correctly, this conversation was intended to be for my benefit, because it was vaguely known to my friend and her family that at school I was studying English Literature and I liked writing. A job in insurance was being recommended to me and was reckoned to be right up my street! Well, it is true that John and I have both had moments in our career when we have become involved in drafting or interpreting insurance policy wordings. "Whereas, Hereinafter and Notwithstanding the Foregoing …" as Eeyore might have said. But if you ask me, when it comes to creative writing in insurance, the people with the greatest skills are not John and myself. No, most assuredly, the best works of fiction and imagination come from the clients who send us claims under the policies!

CITY CARTOONS

City of London cartoon comedy: WK Haselden, HM Bateman, 'Alex', 'Bristow'.

Did you know that one of the twentieth-century's most famous cartoonists began his working life as a Lloyd's underwriter? His name was WK Haselden. Don't worry if you have never heard of him: his prime time was a whole century ago. He was recruited by the Daily Mirror in 1904, after which time his cartoons and caricatures became a well-known and instantly recognisable feature of British newspaper-reading. Although WK had never felt suited to a career in insurance and couldn't wait to turn his back on it, his time working at Lloyd's did him one big favour: it was his drawing of George Faber, a prominent Lloyd's underwriter, that caught the eye of the Daily Mirror's editor.

Well done whoever it was at Lloyd's who had the bright idea of commissioning the great cartoonist HM Bateman to pen his series of wonderful cartoon drawings 'Laughter at Lloyd's' in the mid-1920s. In a trademark Bateman cartoon, usually featuring high society at work or play, the humour derived from someone displaying Bad Form – breaching social etiquette: 'The Man Who Threw a Snowball at St Moritz'; 'The Man Who Lit a Cigar Before the Royal Toast', etc. Those looking on would over-react with apoplectic body language: goggling and exclaiming with horror; necks bulging; spectacles flying off their noses.

Bateman's cartoons endure as a vivid and vital pictorial slice of Lloyd's of London history. Lloyd's at that time was a bastion of male chauvinism, privilege and snobbery, and Bateman captured this utterly. All his drawings depicted the familiar interior of the Room: the Lutine Bell, the Rostrum, the Lloyd's waiters in their traditional red coats and black top hats. 'The Underwriter Who Missed the Total Loss' is one of the best known and funniest of the series. The underwriter is depicted crowing and jumping for joy – there is a sub-plot here that any showing of emotion would be *ipso facto* frowned upon, in the Room – while all the rival underwriters who wrote the fatal policy stand and fume at him, or collapse on to the floor in wailing despair. In a partner cartoon, 'The Underwriter Who Never Missed a Total Loss' creeps miserably out through the door, clad in a threadbare old raincoat.

Today we view those Bateman cartoons with our extra dimension of hindsight: the Lloyd's and London insurance market is much more egalitarian now; moreover, you couldn't replicate some of Bateman's scenes like 'The Lloyd's Broker Furtively Entering a Small Company's Office to Finish His Risk'. In former times yes it was *infra dig* for a bluechip Lloyd's broker to do such a thing: it was the equivalent of taking his Rolls Royce to be serviced at Arthur Daley's lock-up instead of the main dealers in Park Lane. But long since, the market has evolved and if suitable financial security is demonstrated, companies can and do compete with and share business with Lloyd's, without being looked down upon (That said, some of the old snobbery still reigned as recently as the early 1990s when I can remember the haughty chief underwriter of a medium-sized Lloyd's syndicate absurdly using the term "fringe company" to describe a giant global insurance company that was sharing a risk with him.)

The Daily Telegraph knew that they were on to a winner in 1992 when they poached the 'Alex' cartoon strip from The Independent newspaper. The artful and arrogant Alex, created by the writers Charles Peattie and Russell Taylor, is still going strong today. I'd warrant that if you'd like to study the history of the City of London during the last quarter of a century, a wander through the Alex cartoons might be more rewarding and instructive than some dry old text-book. Alex has always been topical: the storylines have included thinly-disguised references to contemporary big scandals in the real world (Nick Leeson, Northern Rock, etc) and have faithfully reflected market cycles being upbeat (cue ostentatious over-spending and hedonism) or in recession (cue frenzied efforts to get round expense-cutting, or, in uncanny echo of Bateman's 'Furtive Broker' cartoon, shame at having to scrabble for small-money deals that MegaBank would have disdained in more prosperous times).

In the swagger of the new money-markets, bringing derivatives-traders and big-bonus earners in their wake, an early Alex cartoon had him declaring: "How many twenty-five year olds own a brand-new BMW?" I can date precisely my own first awareness of these brash new usurpers in the City: when my company moved to a new office building in 1986, where the other occupied floor had the nameplate of a merchant bank, we found that their section of the car-park was full of Porsches. There was a rumour that they had only rented a floor of the building for the purpose of gaining car-parking space in the City: even if that was exaggerated, it illustrated the new profligacy of the time. Picking up on the Essex Boy theme, an Alex cartoon had Alex and his snooty Mergers & Acquisitions colleagues competing against "those spivs and wide boys from the Moneybroking Department" in a company paintball match: in the punch-line Alex instructed Clive: "Don't shoot till you see the whites of their socks!"

Of course, the most shocking element of the Alex cartoons – the deliberate, confrontational and outrageous humour – is the complete absence of business ethics or recognition that greedy, obnoxious behaviour is anything other than normal. Alex and his male buddies are horrendously sexist, too. It is given that the females encountered in their business world are either bimbos or totty, or, worse still, attracting the highest degree of scorn, they are power-dressing female executives. One imagines that Alex would nod in approval if you told him that when the Daily Mirror was founded in 1903 it was originally as a women's newspaper, employing only female journalists, but it was a flop, and within months they were all sacked. But oh! – for the 'Bristow' cartoon of an earlier age, when the author Frank Dickens allowed his bowler-hatted and pinstripe-suited anti-hero to at least be nice to the tea ladies or the ladies that watered the flowers, in the office.

I would like, self-righteously and perhaps naively, to divest the

London insurance market from the perceived immorality and social uselessness of the money markets: "divest" is a good word, for some thirty years ago in a process of self-regulation all Lloyd's brokers divested any ownership they had of Lloyd's syndicates, thus freeing themselves from conflict of interest. One can't imagine Alex and his cohorts voluntarily doing likewise. I prefer Alex when the gentler humour and clever word-play has him escaping temporarily into Narnia. There, he and Clive meet a Call-Centaur; a statue turned to stone by the White Witch is mocked because it's a city trader from the early days when mobile phones were the size of bread-loaves. Best of all, and something that I can't deny might happen in insurance, while crawling through the wardrobe to find their way into Narnia, Alex and Clive have the presence of mind to take two jackets off the hangers and slip back to the office to put the jackets on the backs of their chairs while they are away!

WHAT'S IN A (LLOYD'S) NAME?

There was an outcry in 1963 when Euston railway station was rebuilt, and the grand Doric arch was demolished and removed from the entrance. Conservationists fought bitterly to try and save it, but the modernists won the day with their argument that the huge stone arch (built in 1837) served no useful purpose and would look unsightly if it remained a part of the swish new building that was promised.

Lloyd's of London insurance went the opposite way when they unveiled their new superstructure building in 1986. They decided to preserve something from the past. The committee ordained that the architect (Richard Rogers) and the developers (Bovis) should incorporate the magnificent stone façade of the old 1925 Lloyd's building into their design-and-build of the new headquarters.

The visual result of this for Lloyd's was a violent and some would say disastrous clash of old and new architecture. There isn't a problem if you observe the Lloyd's building from the Lime Street side. From there it all looks shiny, metallic and modern ("like an oil-rig", is a common reaction from first-time visitors). However, if you stand in Leadenhall Street to look at the frontage of the Lloyd's building, there is no denying that it looks rather weird to see the carved stone façade that masks the first few floors of the new building, to the far right.

Was it really a good idea for Lloyd's to hang on to the old façade? I have mixed feelings about it. However, the thing that really fascinates me is the stroke of luck for the 1925 Committee of Lloyd's that their twelve personal names have become so visibly preserved for posterity. Every day when I walk past the entrance-way at this north-west corner of the Lloyd's building my eye is drawn to the list of twelve names engraved into the stone base:

PERCY GRAHAM McKINNON;

EUSTACE RALPH PULBROOK;
etc, etc.

It's jolly fine for those particular gentlemen that their names remain on prominent display in 2013; but, the question might reasonably be asked: what did they each do in their lifetimes to make themselves more deserving of such fame in perpetuity than any of the other committee members of Lloyd's of London throughout the institution's 300-year reign? Why, for example, is there no visible tribute, externally, to the legendary Cuthbert Heath of the early twentieth-century or to giants of eighteenth-century past such as John Julius Angerstein and John Bennett, whereas WILFRID BOUGHTON ROUSE (to choose one name at random) can still announce his 1925 badge-of-office to the present-day world?

In fairness, two of the "Class of '25" indelibly belong in the very top tier of late and greats of Lloyd's history. By 1925, ARTHUR LLOYD STURGE had already served a term as Chairman of Lloyd's, and what a dramatic time he had presided over. In addition to organising the move from the cramped old underwriting room at the Royal Exchange, securing in 1923 the new site on Leadenhall Street occupied formerly by the East India Insurance Company, Sturge acted controversially but decisively in 1923 when it was realised that a syndicate named Harrison had been writing unsound motor credit insurance, and was heading for failure.

Decreeing that the whole reputation of Lloyd's was at stake, and that policyholders of the Harrison syndicate must have their liabilities met in full, Sturge demanded from the rest of the Lloyd's market a voluntary whip-round of circa £400,000 – a massive sum for those days. (Buying the land at East India Avenue had cost £500,000). It was not quite the first bail-out in Lloyd's history, but at that time it was by far the biggest.

EUSTACE RALPH PULBROOK grasped another big nettle when

he was Chairman of Lloyd's during World War Two. Fearing a German invasion of Britain, and the seizure of Lloyd's policy documentation that would disclose details and locations of key USA military or industrial enterprises, the USA authorities declared that insurance with Lloyd's of London could not continue. This was a huge crisis for Lloyd's, who derived a large premium income from the USA. Pulbrook flew across the Atlantic in 1942 (a brave feat in itself) and negotiated a clever solution. In effect, Lloyd's underwriters would insure American companies "blind": the policy documents issued in London would contain no identifying name or information, but instead would show a reference number that would link to the full policy, held temporarily in a new clearing-house established in New York for the duration of the war. By that stroke of genius alone, Sir Eustace Pulbrook can be lauded as a saint and saviour of Lloyd's.

"What's in a Name?" I make a deliberate play-on-words here, for in Lloyd's parlance a "Name" in the old days was an individual person who pledged his or her assets to a particular syndicate, to provide underwriting capital. I make another little play-on-words, too. In the days that I speak of, most syndicates traditionally were known by the name of the chief underwriter. Simple enough, one might think; but, perversely, many people working in the Room (as the trading area of Lloyd's is called) would instead refer to a syndicate by the name of its former chief underwriter, or even the one before that. This practice might be likened to cockney rhyming-slang: its effect was to confuse newcomers and outsiders, who could hardly be expected to know immediately that Cockell was the same as Rouse, or that Lark and Gibbs had followed on from Roylance.

Motor insurance syndicates at Lloyd's, incidentally, preferred to take abstract names such as Paladin and Red Star. That trend has spread now throughout the new so-called "corporate" Lloyd's, where most of the syndicates have brand names traversing the alphabet from Ace to XL; although a few such as Beasley and

Catlin bear the personal name of their founding chief underwriter.

I wrote earlier that each time I walk past the giant stone portal of the 1925 Lloyd's building I see the twelve names of the 1925 Committee, inscribed there. However, this has recently become a half-truth. Modern practicality has now outranked pomp and dignity. What do I mean by this? Simply that a portable 'No Smoking' sign is now manually planted on the steps outside the entrance, during work-day hours. This sign obscures most of the twelve names. On the opposite side of the entrance another such sign blots out the inscription stating that His Majesty King George V laid the foundation stone in 1925. Oh dear, no longer much majesty for His Majesty.

At the end of the 1980s, Lloyd's was in crisis when its Names suffered catastrophic underwriting losses. The rescue plan saw in effect the creation of a "good" bank (new Lloyd's, largely with corporate investment) and "bad" bank (Equitas, firewalling all the toxic business).

Picking up on the widely-publicised allegations of incompetence and skulduggery, 'Private Eye' magazine had a field-day with its 'Lloyd's Rhyming Slang': Annual Loss – Not for the Boss; Fishy Smell – Lutine Bell; Huge Claims – Names; Oil Spill – Massive Bill; Hurricane Hugo – End to Cash Flow; Underwriter – Two Billion Lighter; Sell the Jag – Bit of a Drag.

And this excellent poem was penned by John Preston:

(To the tune: 'There is Nothing Like a Dame')

We've got brokers, cover-holders, reinsurers by the score;
We've got underwriters waiting on the underwriting floor;
We've attorneys and adjusters sitting waiting for the claims;
What ain't we got? We ain't got Names.

There is nothing like a Name:
Nothing in the world. There is nothing in this game that is anything like a Name.
Nothing makes like a Name; nothing takes like a Name; then nothing shakes like a
Name,
And nothing breaks like a Name. There's not a thing that starts off with so much cash
And ends up giving to Equitas:
A gentle, vulnerable, greedy gullible Name.

TOWER 42

What is the collective noun for cranes? A "cluster of cranes" – a "conglomeration of cranes" - a "crowd of cranes" – or simply where I started: a "collection of cranes"?

Throughout my working career in the City it has always been a sure bet that as my commuter train approaches London Bridge railway station I will see cranes peppering the far horizon of the City of London across the Thames. It doesn't seem to matter whether the economy is in "boom" or "bust": the great Mammon of property development never seems to take a rest.

For example, at the start of 2012 if you had chosen to stand in Leadenhall Street and crane your neck (sorry) to look across to the Tower 42 building on the far side of Bishopsgate, you'd have seen a veritable "Crane City". In the foreground, the Aon Building (nicknamed "The Cheesegrater") was starting to reach for the sky; behind it the prospective Bishopsgate Tower (or "Pinnacle") offered further evidence that the skyscraper stampede was in full throttle in this and in many other parts of the City, notwithstanding the economy being in recession.

January 2012: Early construction of the new Aon Building in Leadenhall Street, with the Tower 42 building in the background.

As regards that particular vantage point in Leadenhall Street it was as though the wagons are circling the Lloyd's of London insurance building: by this I mean that if a company wants to make a very visible statement of its important size and influence in the London insurance and reinsurance market, why not plant its headquarters next door to the Lloyd's building, in as tall and striking a building as the planning authorities will allow? Willis, one of the major broking firms, boldly built a shiny brand new office block in Lime Street for the New Millennium, and it now comes to pass that Aon, another of the broking giants, will not only occupy land in "Crane City" but will move its corporate seat from the USA to London.

As my own career in the City began to count down towards my retirement date I couldn't help noticing that my Monday to Friday on-foot commute between Cannon Street railway station and my office had become an almost intolerable obstacle-race as more and more streets and pavements became blocked up by building lorries, scaffolding and temporary walkways for pedestrians. Admittedly, some of this disruption was caused by the necessary evil of a large-scale replacement of old and worn-out Victorian pipework beneath the City; mostly, though, old banks and similar types of buildings were being ripped down and replaced by more modern ones, or were undergoing change of use into hotels, shops or restaurants and bars.

During the many months of 2011 and 2012 when I had to thread my way precariously past building sites in the City, trying to guard my clothes and shoes from dust, mud and puddles, it got so bad that I even began to doubt my enjoyment of the excellent poem by Thom Gunn (one of my favourite poets) superbly describing a downtown construction site in the USA where "big cranes jut" and builders display their astonishing ability to stride across girders with the confidence and poise of a cat.

Tower 42 was once the City of London's tallest building, and was originally called the Natwest Tower. It was in 1981, just over thirty years ago, that the mighty Natwest Tower stretched to the highest height of the City of London skyline, proclaiming itself as a symbol of the power and grandeur of the Natwest Bank. Alas the fortunes of the poor old Natwest Bank and its iconic London headquarters would spiral down after that. There were adverse trading losses during the 1980s. Awkward questions began to be asked about the wisdom of having spent so much money on building its plush new headquarters. The bank tottered out of that crisis, but then in 1993 an IRA bomb caused extensive damage to the Tower, and it ended up being sold. The new owners rechristened it as Tower 42 – named after the number of floors.

After another series of trading disasters during the late 1990s the Natwest Bank was gobbled up by RBS. The Natwest Tower was reincarnated as Tower 42 but the uncomfortable indignity is that tourists nowadays largely ignore it, and literally turn their back on it, as they flock eagerly to photograph and be photographed next to "The Gherkin", the eye-catching Swiss Re glass-tower in St Mary Axe.

The 44-storey Heron Tower in Bishopsgate, erected in 2011, ended Tower 42's thirty-year reign as tallest building in the City of London. Since then "The Shard" has filled the horizon next to London Bridge on the south of the river, and seems to be sufficiently and intimidatingly tall that it may put an end to the giant London skyscraper game of "leapfrog" for a very long time indeed.

Am I the only person who is wondering how all this new commercial space will be filled, when we are told that the march of e-technology will enable more and more remote working? (Cue the old joke about the head of a giant Japanese electronics corporation who crowned his successful reign by putting the company building up for sale so that they could find somewhere smaller). But new-builds like Heron Tower and the "The Shard" are part-residential, so maybe that answers my question.

A vision comes into my head: one of Magritte's most famous paintings, in which the sky is filled with men in dark raincoats and bowler hats, all floating in mid-air. If we keep getting large new buildings in the City, creating extra wind-traps at street level, on gale-force days will we all suddenly be levitated up into the sky, to hover in suspended animation where we can marvel at all the glass and steel edifices that stretch far away, below?

CITY LITERARY

The new Artizan Street Library opened in the City of London in December 2012. Susan, Jo and Cathy are in the photo.

LLOYD'S LOG

Writing in his famous diary, Samuel Pepys recorded a "Doh!" moment when his honesty cost him money. He was offered a line on an overdue policy for a ship that was thought to be at sea. Pepys happened to know that it was safely in port. But instead of concealing his information and pocketing the premium from a safe bet: "Like an ass, I told the Alderman."

For the underwriter assessing risk, there is nowadays a ready availability of global information, news and data – some of it via new technology and software (catastrophe modelling, analytics.) But for the early marine underwriters at Lloyd's it was very different. News travelled slowly and was often unreliable. If you walk down St Michael's Alley, off Cornhill, you'll find the Jamaica Inn and a wall-plaque identifying the site of the very first coffee house in the City of London in 1652. It became a recognised place of business, such that letters from anywhere in the world, addressed simply to "The Jamaica, London" could be relied upon to arrive.

By 1700, the daily working life of a City of London merchant would be this: "Worked in his counting house till 8am; breakfasted on toast and Cheshire cheese; spent two hours in his shoppe; went to a coffee house for news; dined on a thundering joint; looked in on 'Change; went to Lloyd's coffee house for business; moved on to another coffee house for recreation; went to a sack-shop to drink with acquaintants." By then, Edward Lloyd had recognised the importance of reporting the shipping news. His own attempted newspaper the 'Lloyd's News' had quickly failed in 1696, for his maritime despatches – usually more naval than commercial – came only from a few scattered English ports whereas the rival 'Flying Post' boasted that "divers eminent merchants in the City" relied on its daily presentation of maritime news from as far afield as Amsterdam, Copenhagen, Hague, Namur, Pignerol, Venice and Warsaw.

In 1930 one Edward G Chapman, an assistant underwriter with a Lloyd's syndicate, decided to start up a market magazine. He rather cheekily called it the Lloyd's Official Gazette: in no time at all it was colloquially referred to as the Log, as had no doubt been intended, to capture the Lloyd's shipping association with that word. I know this history of the 'Lloyd's Log' (as became the magazine's official name, eventually) because I have in front of me an absorbing if rather quaint little book 'Tales from the Coffee House – Stories About Lloyd's' authored by William Charles Crocker and published in 1973. From these reminisces one can deduce that the early issues of 'Lloyd's Log' (printed on a duplicating machine and stapled by Mr Chapman's own hands) were something akin to a church magazine: they carried reports of the Lloyd's art society and various sporting groups and activities.

In 1940 the Committee of Lloyd's adopted the 'Lloyd's Log' as a quasi-official publication. One of its most popular features was the page of mathematical puzzles contributed by Mr WG Gooda of Lloyd's each month: it sounds like a bit of a Busman's Holiday to me, to want to solve maths problems after a day in the office calculating marine cargo rates and profit commissions; but as recorded by William Crocker: in 1944 a special 'Lloyd's Log' issue of Mr Gooda's "treacherous" puzzles had a print run of three thousand copies, such was its popularity in wartime when boredom was hard to combat. Returning to Lloyd's after the Allied Landings, a clerk recounted that while dug in on Anzio beach, pinned down by enemy fire, he and his fellow troops had found the Gooda book a "Godsend" to help pass the time.

William Crocker aimed in his book to present a series of light and humorous word-sketches of Lloyd's underwriters and underwriting. This he duly did, but for me some of the "humour" is so stodgy that I might have guessed 1873 rather than 1973 to have been the book's date of publication. To be fair to the author, he was writing in the idiom of "old Lloyd's" – by which I mean pre-war: he evidently belonged to the Huntin', Shootin' and Fishin' social set; his name-dropping abounded with double-barrelled surnames, Colonel this and Major that. I am just about old enough to remember hearing about Gardner Mountain & D'Ambrumenil, also Hartley Cooper, and certainly Sam Meacock who came to Lloyd's in 1873 and was regarded as Father of the House when the young William Crocker began working there and extracted anecdotes about Mr Meacock's childhood perching on the farm gate and watching the Bath Mail Coach drive through his village. And where was this hamlet, where open fields stretched in all directions save for the odd barn or two? Hammersmith!

William Crocker, later knighted, was a lawyer by profession. He handled many high profile insurance cases: arson, jewel theft, etc. I can't pretend that modern readers would likely find his 'Stories About Lloyd's' to be side-splittingly funny, but I did like the tale of the missing yacht *The Bride* that slipped anchor while its young and amateur crew were larking about onshore. Lloyd's circulated its agents and against all odds a few days later its Belfast correspondent spotted a yacht of that name beside the quay. But was it the right yacht? The agent cabled the owner: "Does *The Bride* have a red bottom?" All well and good, you might imagine, except that the owner, a middle-aged bachelor, had in late life suddenly taken a wife, and it was she, on return from the honeymoon, who had first read the telegram ...

The 'Lloyd's Log' was published for many years (Mr Gooda's page for twenty-seven years) but today if you *log* on to the Lloyd's website you'll inevitably find instead a Lloyd's *Blog* ...Today, marine business accounts for much of the enduring visible history of Lloyd's. The ritual ringing of the Lutine Bell derives from a shipwreck in 1799. The ledger page containing news of the sinking of the *Titanic* in 1912 is kept on prominent display, and the Nelson Room has a wealth of maritime exhibits for visitors to see. Meanwhile the daily newspaper 'Lloyd's List' has run uninterrupted since 1734: in conjunction with the 'Shipping Index' it was the marine market's Bible. More general publications also serve the London market: 'Insurance Day', 'Insurance Insider' and

'Post Magazine' are regular standbys, while the excellent 'Business Insurance' reports from the USA. Magazines such as 'ReInsurance' and 'The Review' fill the specialist roles. I sometimes wonder what might happen if the tabloid press decided to come in: would phones be hacked to get a searing exposé of what the Committee of Lloyd's really thinks about Solvency 2; would the front page be filled with "cheesecake" photos of glamorous young starlets for whom tenuous links to Lloyd's would be claimed, such as her brother lives next door to an LMX broker who works for Aon? Perish the thought.

Harking back to that merchants' diary of 1700 I note that a pub named the Cheshire Cheese is still in the City of London today. Thinking also of Pepys and his honesty, I note that others of his time were not so scrupulous. When a ship the *Vansittart* was lost in 1717, the owners found that their insurance was £200 short: the broker had scribbled some false names on the cover note and had run off with the premium. That broker comes to mind when I am riding on the DLR from Shadwell to Bank, for the train passes a pub named The Artful Dodger!

LONDON'S EVENING NEWSPAPERS

In 'The Blue Carbuncle' – my favourite of the Sherlock Holmes short stories – Holmes decides upon a ruse to try and trap a jewel thief. He commands Peterson, the commissionaire of the apartment block at 221B Baker Street, to place an advertisement in the London evening newspapers. He goes on to name an abundance of them: the Globe, Star, Pall Mall, St James's Gazette, Evening News, Standard, Echo plus any others that the sender can think of.

That is certainly a throwback to late Victorian times, when London commuters such as Charles Pooter had plenty of choice if they wanted to purchase an evening newspaper to read on the train home to Holloway. Nowadays in London, the one and only option is the (free) Evening Standard.

One of my daily small pleasures is to pore over the latest chess puzzle set for readers by the perennial and worthy Leonard Barden, who – amazingly - has been editing the column since 1956.

Mr Barden's chess puzzle is nowadays only found on-line in the Evening Standard. It has been dropped from the printed newspaper version. I suppose this echoes the recent declining number of active chess players in Britain: the rise of multiple rival hand-held or keyboard computer-games has evidently diluted the membership of chess clubs because less people are getting addicted to the game.

Most commuters these days, morning and night, appear to be Sudoku addicts. This Japanese numbers-game achieved instant mass popularity when some British newspapers first tested it with readers a few years ago. I belong now to a minority of die-hards who still do crossword puzzles on the train. Add to that the new phenomena of e-books (Kindle), i-pods and mobile phones, and you can safely say that the pastimes engaged in by London commuters during bus, train and tube rides have been revolutionised since I first started work in 1966.

Give it a few more years and maybe there will be no "paper" newspapers any more: everyone will be getting his or her "fix" of the national news, celebrity love-lives, Sudoku or what-have-you by simply reading a hand-held electronic device. Should that become the norm, it will no doubt be a great relief to the bus, train and tube staff whose job it is, every rush-hour morning and night, to clear away the numerous abandoned giveaway newspapers that passengers routinely leave on the seats, floors and luggage-racks. It reminds me of the days when James Goldsmith, arch-enemy of 'Private Eye' magazine, launched his new magazine 'Now!'. It was mercilessly lampooned in 'Private Eye', who re-christened it as 'Talbot!' and had a merry time inventing lots of imaginary uses for the hundreds of bales of unsold copies that they insisted were clogging up newsagents' storerooms throughout the country.

Crosswords! One of my very earliest memories of my childhood is eagerly waiting for my Dad to come home from work, so that I could have the children's puzzle page in the Evening News. I liked best the picture-crossword. I was to find during my broking career in Lloyd's that it was the convention on many of the underwriting boxes that The Times and the Daily Telegraph crosswords should be completed during the ritual mid-morning coffee-break in the Captain's Room. It was there that I gained the essential knowledge (mainly from the staff of Frank Green & Others, Syndicate 860) that any reference to a sailor in a crossword clue will likely mean a "tar" or "AB" (able-bodied). I learned that a "flower" won't mean a daisy or a tulip: it will mean the Danube or the Thames; likewise, "butter" will have nothing to do with a dairy: it will mean a stag or a ram.

While I was still living with my parents in the late 1960s my favourite columnist in the Evening News was the Earl of Arran. He seemed always to pen lucid and pithy observations about life, such that you would want to send a copy of his weekly column to our Prime Minister and say: "Yes! Why don't we run the country like this!"

I suspect that the liberal views of the Eighth Earl of Arran would not have found favour with the institution known to many Cannon Street commuters as "Sean Millwall". A regular fixture just outside the station entrance for many years, Sean sold the evening papers from his pitch that he usually decorated with the Union Jack flag. If it was St George's Day you could depend upon him rigging up his newsstand with a gramophone that would blare out 'Land of Hope and Glory'; he would also make collections for charity or for British troops. His excellent sales gimmick was to make witty handwritten alterations to the news placards. Two separate headlines "Westminster Crisis for Blair" and 'Shop-Lifting Vicar Jailed' would likely be juxtaposed by Sean to read: "Blair Jailed for Shop-Lifting"!

Let me return to Sherlock Holmes. He sometimes found his way from Baker Street to the City of London – for example when visiting an opium den behind the wharves at London Bridge in the story of 'The Man with the Twisted Lip'.

The strange case of 'The Red-Headed League' took Holmes to Aldersgate in EC1. You may remember that his disgruntled client complained that he had been engaged to sit at a desk, copying out the Encyclopaedia Britannica. At four sovereigns a week, the wages were good, but the job abruptly ended, without warning, when the office door was found locked one morning.

Hmm ... stuck in a London office day after day, doing boring, repetitive and pointless work? I'm not sure that Holmes's client had much to complain about, really? He only had to do it for eight weeks. I know someone who might argue that he had to do that for forty-six years!

SAVE OUR LIBRARIES!

"To lose <u>one</u> library is unfortunate; to lose <u>two</u>, Mr Dowlen, is careless!"

Fair comment - but the fact remains that during the early months of the year 2011, I did "lose" two libraries! The one in my home town of Orpington closed, and so did the one in Camomile Street, near the office where I work in the City of London.

It wasn't quite as drastic as I have stated it above. Each of the two libraries was scheduled to relocate to a brand new (albeit smaller) modern building. The one in Orpington swiftly did so, after only a two-week shutdown. So it wasn't long before I was back to terrorise the long-suffering Orpington library staff with more of my habitual S.O.S. calls at their enquiry desk ("I've forgotten who wrote 'Lorna Doone'?"; "Can you check if any books are overdue on my wife's ticket?"; "There used to be a book in the local history section with a red cover, about urban development, but I can't see it there now?")... (In answer to the latter question, the obliging lady member of staff would politely find the book for me within fifteen seconds, demonstrating that it was there right in front of my eyes all the time).

There was a much longer delay in restoring a library to me and to fellow office workers and residents of London EC3. It was classic Nonsense from the World of Lewis Carroll: shortly after closure of the Camomile Street building the City of London Libraries website announced the name of the street in which the replacement library would be located, but further investigation revealed that the specified building in that street didn't actually exist. It reminded me of 'Alice Through the Looking Glass' and the episode in which Alice enters a shop and sees that it is stacked full of goods for sale, but whenever she tries to focus her gaze on any particular shelf, that shelf instantly becomes empty!

Patience is a virtue, though: the second-to-last week of

September 2011 ushered in the novelty of a brand new mobile library van for our delight and delectation in London EC3! There came simultaneously the news that the promised new permanent building would be ready for occupation in October 2012. A whole year more to wait ... but in the meantime we could climb aboard the Big White Bus and borrow a few books at least, from the cramped interior of the mobile library where the words "swing" and "cat" came instantly to mind!

Along with the thrill of my having not one, but two new, modern, spick and span library premises to inspect, there came the wistfulness of bidding farewell to buildings old.

In Orpington, our former library was housed inside the medieval wooden-beamed splendour of The Priory buildings and gardens. A visit there to borrow books was a multi-cultural experience: not only a flowers-and-shrubs horticultural treat outdoors but an absorbing treat indoors if one had time to browse the rooms and displays of the London Borough of Bromley Museum housed inside The Priory too.

The lending library in Camomile Street was never, I admit, one to set the pulse racing for architectural or aesthetic pleasure. Nevertheless after a few weeks I felt an inexplicable nostalgia for its featureless large room on the ground floor: it seems to have happened too abruptly during the spring and summer of 2011 that the whole huge building has been mercilessly swaddled in scaffolding and gauze, and then suddenly with a swish! of the magician's cloth, it has all disappeared, opening up a big new expanse of sky behind Bishopsgate.

But that's the modern construction industry: buildings can and do disappear frighteningly fast, these days; and the new ones seem to fly up in the blink of an eye, almost as if the yellow-helmeted construction workers empty the contents of a bottle of Grow-More on to the foundations last thing on a Friday afternoon, and by the time they return the next Monday morning, another ten stories of steel and glass have sprouted up towards the sky.

Save our Libraries! – Government Cuts

Inevitably, the recent changes affecting the Orpington and Camomile Street libraries have some crossover with the cuts in public spending that are currently being threatened or have already been imposed by the government during the recession.

The above statement doesn't explain the full circumstances that have brought about the relocations of the Orpington and the Camomile Street library, but the savage spectre of library closures has sent out shock waves that continue to reverberate and to cause anxieties in our towns and shires where people don't want to lose their precious libraries.

It is a tough coincidence for public libraries throughout the whole country that the sudden pressure on them to justify their existence has come at a time when e-commerce and e-technology is dramatically revolutionising the world of books. Authors, publishers and booksellers are being forced to reinvent themselves if they are to survive and thrive. Libraries too have come under the spotlight as local Councils evaluate the fast-changing dynamics of why ratepayers would still use a public library, now that e-technology has radically altered so many of our social habits.

What scope is there for public libraries to add new strings to their bows? I mean: additional to books (for borrowing &/or reference), reading-rooms for newspapers and periodicals, and internet facilities? I'm sure that public libraries are getting the message that the more they can engage with their local community, the better their chances of lasting the course. Lately on my travels I have spotted a good few libraries escalating their range of customer-attracting activities to the best extent that they can within budgetary and space restraints. And why not? To hell with tradition: if a library can offer a public service (or more than one) that it didn't offer before, of tangible benefit and not just a gimmick, that is surely good evolution.

Finally, I don't mean to marginalise books. If we are to Save Our Libraries! we must celebrate Books! Books! Books! The library staff responsible for choosing the books for Orpington and London EC3 (mobile van) rose admirably to the challenge. They took an assured stride into the second decade of the New Millennium by offering in each new library a skilfully selected and attractively presented array of crisp and bright new books. If more people are attracted into public libraries and they come to realise that they can be enriched by books, I believe that this above all will help to Save Our Libraries.

I am pleased to conclude by giving you the information that the new Artizan Street Library and Community Centre did indeed open in the City of London in December 2012. Conveniently situated five minutes' walk from the Aldgate and Liverpool Street underground stations, it is well worth a visit.

SPEAKER'S CORNER AT TOWER HILL

A lunch hour stroll in November 2009.

Taking a lunch hour stroll through Tower Hill and down to the Thames pier on a bright and sunny day in early November, I find that my mood is unusually nostalgic.

Part of the blame for this, I decide, can be attributed to my old friend Michael Gould who has sent me his written impressions of a recent visit to London. Travelling up by train from his home in Whitstable, Michael had taken the opportunity to walk along some of the London streets that were familiar to him when he worked in the old Customs building on Lower Thames Street. Unsurprisingly after an absence of some thirty years, he had noticed plenty of change – especially the large preponderance of new (well, new to him) high-rise buildings all around.

A quick glance at the calendar supplies me with the other reason for my brooding upon times past. The date reads 4 November 2009. Four days on from my sixty-second birthday, I am still working as a nine-to-five London commuter, but Father Time has given me a hefty nudge to remind me that my day of retirement draws ever closer. Last night on my doormat at home I found a letter from one of my pension providers, inviting me to start drawing some of my retirement income if I wish to do so.

Let me deal with Michael's reflections first. I pause halfway down Tower Hill, noticing, as Michael also did, "the vast number of tourists walking about." To me this is not a new phenomenon; nor am I astonished that "everywhere there are smart plants and elegant chairs to sit in, and newly painted railings." However, I must acknowledge that Michael will inevitably picture Tower Hill in its former dilapidated and unkempt condition. He will not have observed, as I have done, its recent transformation into a glazed, neatly-ordered and spacious plaza. They stage summer concerts here now, featuring top-selling artistes from the world of music and theatre. Even the Beefeaters have joined the rest of us in the twenty-first century, for our newspapers now inform us that female members of the Yeoman (Yeoperson?) staff have alleged that misdeeds of harassment and discrimination have been perpetrated upon them in the workplace.

In his travelogue sent to me the previous week Michael had wistfully remembered when Tower Hill served as a Speaker's Corner, offering open-air entertainment for whatever audience cared to linger and listen to such of the speeches that were audible above the noise of traffic. "Donald Soper, where are you now?" beseeched Michael, in his letter to me.

Ah, yes, I think to myself, I do recall that in former times when I passed by Tower Hill I would occasionally notice some shouting and gesticulating. If I went over to take a closer look, it was usually the case that I couldn't make out much of what was being said, but it was an amusing diversion if I had a few minutes to spare. Am I correct in thinking that there used to be street theatre too, sometimes? - fire-eaters, or escapologists freeing themselves from chains?

By now, I have sauntered towards the top of the Tower Hill precinct. Almost as if by command, an evangelist grabs my attention. "AND JESUS SAID UNTO US …" Startled, I look in the direction of his loudly-uttered words. It is not hard to spot him. A tall, dark-skinned and grey-haired man is standing by the back wall of All-Hallows Church, declaiming the gospel. He holds in both hands a large hardback Bible, although his eyes are cast heavenwards and he seems not to be reading from the open page.

My immediate instinct is to send a text message to Michael: "Guess what! Speaker's Corner is alive and well at Tower Hill!" Hmm – on second thoughts, it's alive but it's not particularly well. No one is taking any notice of the self-appointed orator. At pavement level, he is at some disadvantage. In the old days, the speakers thundered forth from an elevated and railed-off platform that looked out towards the river. The site is still there today, but when I glance up at it I see that a young policewoman is patrolling it, with walkie-talkie in hand and a determined frown on her face.

This seems a rather over-the-top deployment of police resources, I muse to myself. Are the government really so frightened of free speech at Tower Hill? Ah well, I suppose if any political activists were allowed to address the lunch hour strollers and tourists, they'd be complaining about western capitalist forces in Iraq and Afghanistan. Back in the 1960s when I would first have encountered the Speaker's Corner at Tower Hill the tub-thumpers would have been railing about Vietnam. And if I had stood in this very same place two hundred years ago, in 1809, someone would no doubt have been saying what a nice chap Napoleon was, and shouldn't the British army leave him alone.

I send Michael a text message anyway. I know how much he would love to be here and to heckle the evangelist. I can picture Michael standing next to me, a friendly grin spreading over his face while eagerly awaiting an opportunity to chip in and verbally challenge the speaker. Thereafter, the two of them would happily go at it hammer and tongs, while the rest of us gradually slipped away to return to our office desks or to view some of the other tourist attractions. Were I to return at dusk, after completing my daily hours of work, I would probably find Michael and the speaker still locked in earnest debate.

Tower Hill is a location that has touched into my working life on several occasions. If I want to nominate somewhere that marks and measures the longevity of my business career in the City of London, and also somewhere that will remind me that my sands of time are starting to run out, Tower Hill is certainly a suitable choice.

I spent twelve years (from 1976) working for a reinsurance broker whose parent company was headquartered at the Bowring building in Tower Place. It was a drab three-storey E-shaped concrete eyesore, evidencing all the worst aspects of 1950s architecture and construction. Mercifully, I never had to work inside it, although I was sometimes required to attend meetings there. The Bowring empire overlapped into some equally nondescript buildings at nearby Sugar Quay, Byward Street and Great Tower Street.

There came later an interlude in my career, lasting some seven weeks in 2007, when I did actually work inside the Bowring building. By this time, the old crumbling concrete edifice had been long demolished, and in its place stood the sleek and glittering new Marsh building, six storeys high. On his day trip to London my friend Michael would have surely counted this imposing glasshouse as one of the brash new intruders into his lost landscape of three decades earlier.

In the bright light of a November early afternoon, taking a skyward glance at the Marsh building, then craning my neck and swivelling my body so that I can also take in the elegant green spire of All Hallows Church, I am put in mind of my late friend and poetry mentor Donald Ward:

> Glassy rooms which disinfect the sky
> Rise in glass until you lose your mind
> In numbed excitement, a sort of hypnotist's eye
> Losing halfway the crowd's or traffic's voice ...

Donald wrote those lines about Gresham Street in London EC2, but I'm sure he would permit my bundling his poem into a taxicab and removing it a mile or so east to Tower Place, EC3.

The stretch of riverfront between London Bridge and Tower Bridge is extremely well known to me. For more than a decade (up till about 2004) I walked along either the north side or the south side every weekday morning and evening, on my way to and from work. When taking the northern option I crossed Tower

Bridge and skirted round the Tower of London, passing through Tower Hill. Standing at Tower Hill today, I recall how well I got to know all the dusty nooks and crannies that lurked beside and beneath the old Bowring building for which I now feel a rather illogical fondness.

During the last two years, my visits to Tower Hill have all been for the same purpose: to spend time with my son during our respective lunch hours. We go to the excellent canteen in his office which is none other than the Marsh building, standing on the site of the old Bowring building. What could be more symbolic of my advancing years, I ask myself, than finding my own son employed by the same company that I worked for when I was his age.

Of course, if I were retired, I could return to Tower Hill whenever I liked. I would be free as a bird (well, apart from the ravens who always have to stay in the Tower). I could go and see the Crown Jewels. More extravagantly still, I could launch an open-air speech! I could collude with Michael beforehand. He could become a secretly-planted stooge amongst the tourists walking past. He could interrupt me and we could start an argument. We could see if we could attract a crowd. Now that really would be like old times at Speaker's Corner in Tower Hill.

LONDON BELLS

Two sticks and an apple,
Ring the bells at Whitechapel.

Old Father Bald Pate,
Ring the bells Aldgate.

Maids in white aprons,
Ring the bells at St Catherine's.

Oranges and lemons,
Ring the bells at St Clement's.

When will you pay me?
Ring the bells at Old Bailey.

When I am rich,
Ring the bells at Shoreditch.

When will that be?
Ring the bells at Stepney.

When I am old,
Ring the great bell at Paul's.

Anon (early 18th-century)

OTHER BOOKS BY JERRY DOWLEN

Football

'Ken Collishaw – Cray Wanderers FC Goalscoring Legend' (2006)

'Forever Amber - Cray Wanderers FC 1860-2010, The History of London's Oldest Football Club' (2011)

Biography

'After Football, Nothing Much Happens' (2004)
Donald Ward: Football Fan, Pacifist and Poet.

Poetry

'Walking to the Office' (2003)

'Lio Lios' (Wave Crest Press, 2007)

The City of London: Wandering and Wondering

Design and Artwork: Trevor Mulligan

Printed by: Catford Print Centre

Front Cover: Mansion House, 2012

Back Cover: Guildhall, 2012